leading
good care

First published in 2015
by Jessica Kingsley Publishers
73 Collier Street
London N1 9BE, UK
and
400 Market Street, Suite 400
Philadelphia, PA 19106, USA

www.jkp.com

Library of Congress Cataloging in Publication Data
Burton, John, 1947-
  Leading good care : the task, heart and art of managing social care / John Burton ; foreword by Debbie
Sorkin.
    pages cm
  Includes index.
  1. Social work administration. I. Title.
  HV41.B878 2015
  361.0068'4--dc23
                            2014028621

British Library Cataloguing in Publication Data
A CIP catalogue record for this book is available from the British Library

ISBN 978 1 84905 551 2
eISBN 978 0 85700 985 2

Printed and bound by Bell & Bain Ltd, Glasgow

With thanks to everyone who has helped, supported and tolerated me during the writing of this book, and most of all to my wife, Sattie Lall Burton, who, like many others, manages social care with energy, humour, commitment, love, and sheer brilliance.

CONTENTS

Foreword by Debbie Sorkin **11**

PREFACE: DRIVING A BUS AND LEADING SOCIAL CARE. 13
An introduction to systems thinking. 13
Systems within systems 14
Adding leadership to management. 16
Why I've written this book and how, I hope, it will help you to
lead good care

Introduction Leading Good Care: The Task, Heart and Art
of Managing Social Care **20**
Creating a systems model 21
Building systems of care from the core task outwards 21
Stories of managers taking the lead 22
The theoretical base 22
Ways of using the book 23
The social care manager's professional development and self-
authorisation. 23
Stories of leading good care 24

Chapter 1 Context and Integration **27**
Your care service in its context. 27
    Care services that are integral to their environment . . **29**
No social care service is 'an island entire of itself' 29
    4Cs home care service **29**
Neighbourhood, community, locality 30
    The Limes as a local resource **30**
Economic context 31
    The Hub: At the centre of community action and activity **33**
Social, cultural and political context 34
Your care service in an international context 35
    The Willows: A therapeutic community within its
    neighbourhood **36**
Your service as a 'social ecology' in a world ecology. 37
Suggestions for discussion and activity 38

Chapter 2 Care, the Core Task **40**
The corruption of the core task 41
    Restoring the core task at The Limes **42**
Standards, quality and compliance 43

Standards are breached at The Willows. **44**

Short-lived pyrotechnics as a distraction from the core task   46

The 'failure demand' trap and diversion   47

Investigating an allegation at The Willows **47**

Demand for excessive record keeping at The Limes. . .   **50**

Finance, administration and 'human resources'.   51

Housekeeping, catering, maintenance   52

The core task is the whole task. **52**

The external pressures and demands from professional bodies and

'improvement agencies'   54

Gloria and 4Cs: Setting up an apprenticeship and training

scheme with a local college. **55**

Defining and holding onto the core task   56

A Trojan horse at The Hub?. **56**

Formative clients: The clients that help to shape and clarify the

core task.   58

Suggestions of ways to use this chapter   59

Chapter 3 Beneath the Surface: The Permanent Underside

of Care **61**

Individual feelings.   61

Working with needs and feelings   63

Loss.   63

Uncontained feelings and the need for containment   64

Containing panic at The Hub **65**

The fear and denial of dependency and vulnerability   66

Containing anxieties in social care organisations.   67

Some common individual, group and organisational defences... .   68

Identifying and dismantling defences at The Limes. . .   **71**

Anti-task processes and defences in the wider system   74

A failure to assess risk at The Willows **79**

Working with what is beneath the surface: Creating the therapeutic

framework to enable your staff to work with loss, frailty and death   86

Establishing a therapeutic foundation and framework   86

Gita designs a staff support structure at The Limes . . .   **87**

Some questions and activities to consider, discuss and use in action

learning sets   92

Chapter 4 Boundary: Where Your Service Interacts with

Its Environment (Outside It) and the Uses of

Boundaries in Leading Care **95**

The concept of boundary   95

What does boundary mean?   96

Boundary decisions are 'key' decisions   98

Entries   99

Staff selection and appointment   99

Staff recruitment and selection at The Limes **100**
Client assessment, acceptance and commitment   101
   Accepting a new client at 4Cs **101**
   Recognising and respecting the client's boundaries . . .   **102**
Exporting risk across boundaries   102
   Commitment **103**
   Blurring the boundaries of responsibility **103**
   The effect on Mrs Smith of breaking her boundaries . .   **104**
   Linking the use or misuse of boundaries to the core task   **104**
Exits   105
   Gill asks a client to leave The Willows **106**
   Reinstating a broken boundary **107**
Partnerships and collaboration   108
   Collaborative working pays off for Mrs Smith **109**
External relationships and reputation   110
   Mrs Smith and The Hub Caps **112**
The use of boundaries   113
   Mrs Smith's boundary issues at The Limes **113**
   The boundary of Ellen's job **113**
   Relaxing and flexing boundaries to meet clients' needs   **115**
Suggestions for exercises, discussion points, group work   116

Chapter 5 Manager as Leader **118**
Lead with values and principles: Believe in what you are doing . .   118
Leading the core task   120
   Mrs Smith and The Hub Club **122**
Involve and support clients in running and evaluating the service .   123
   4Cs' feedback from clients **126**
Communicate   126
   A care worker's choices and decisions **127**
Create and manage resources   133
Lead teams and work across boundaries   137
Promote health and wellbeing   142
Protect people (staff and clients) from exploitation and abuse . . .   145
Working with external audit and inspection   146
   Inspection at The Limes **148**
Lead professional development, including your own   151
   Staff development at 4Cs **151**
   The learning culture at The Willows **152**
Contents of the chapter for discussion   153

**Chapter 6 Changing Place: Turning Barriers to Leadership
        into Enablers and Supporters of Leadership** . .   **156**
Turn it the right way up and it will work   156
Failure demand: The noose that strangles initiative and leadership   157
The problems that trigger failure demand   159

Turning a care service the right way up at 4Cs 160
How Gita took charge of The Limes. 162
How Gill held on to therapeutic community principles at
The Willows 165
How Geoff's leadership is threatened and restored by
group action 166
Converting the barriers to your leadership into supporters. 170
The Careshire Social Care Managers' Network 172
Thinking about this chapter 173

Chapter 7 Stepping Up to Leadership: And Leading Your
Social Care Service with Courage, Vision and
Integrity 174
Stepping up from a low position. 174
Connecting head office with the core task (Gita and
The Limes) 176
Daring to tell the truth and to take the initiative. 177
Courage 178
Vision 179
Integrity and authenticity 179
Resilience 180
Organisation. 180
Leading followers 181
Organising your own supervision 182
Other forms of professional support and development. 182
Joining together in professional groups for change 183
The Careshire Social Care Managers' Network (continued
from Chapter 6) 183

Chapter 8 Afterword. 188

APPENDIX 1: ACTION LEARNING 190
Setting up a network and action learning sets 190

APPENDIX 2: HUMPTY DUMPTY'S SOCIAL CARE WORDS AND PHRASES . . 194
'White van care': 'driving' and 'delivering packages' of
'quality care' 197
Toy train set management 197

BOOKS AND OTHER RESOURCES 201
Books 201
Journals and magazines 203
Websites and newsletters 203
Membership organisations. 203

INDEX 205

FOREWORD

Dame Denise Platt, in her review of adult social care, wrote that 'social care, when delivered well, has the power to transform people's lives'. She was writing in 2007, but her words are as true as ever, and managers in social care are at the heart of that transformation.

This is because social care managers don't just manage along standard lines. Whether working in residential or in home care, the manager's span of responsibilities can be immense, and the range and interconnection of issues with which they have to contend makes their task increasingly complex. Complex issues require leadership, and so social care managers have a key leadership role. It includes not only responsibility for the quality of life of the people they support – the primary task – but also responsibility for the development of their teams; for working productively with their own managers; and for making links with people in healthcare, local authorities, housing and other services so that the service user experiences the best possible quality of care.

This is why leadership is fundamental, and why this book is so welcome. Leadership isn't something that comes with a particular job title or role. It's not confined to managers with the word 'Registered' in their job description, or to Chief Executives. Leadership is for everybody, and it's something everybody can do, and get better at doing. Leadership is about behaviours, and it's embodied and demonstrated every day through a thousand ordinary actions and ways in which we do things. So, there is no good care without good leadership.

This is the central message of *Leading Good Care*. It will take you through what good leadership looks and feels like – for you, for your service users and their families, for your teams and for your organisation. It also reaches out beyond social care, as integration with healthcare makes it more important than ever for managers in the sector to use their leadership effectively and lead beyond the boundaries of their organisation. If you want to step up to leadership, and to lead good care, this book will help you do just that. It's borne of long experience and a passionate belief in the difference good leadership can make. So if you want to transform people's lives, start here.

Debbie Sorkin
National Director of Systems Leadership, The Leadership Centre

PREFACE
DRIVING A BUS AND LEADING SOCIAL CARE

AN INTRODUCTION TO SYSTEMS THINKING

Boarding an overcrowded 109 bus to Brixton (south London) at 8 o'clock in the morning, dinging my pass on the yellow disc, I glance with admiration at the driver. Although she appears to be looking straight ahead, she's checking what's happening on both decks, in the queue at the front door, with the traffic around, whether passengers are trying to sneak aboard through the back door because they can't get on at the front, and deciding when to close the doors because the bus is already seriously overcrowded.

In the space of a few seconds, the driver makes many decisions: whether to stop in the first place; if and when to open the front doors and how many passengers to allow on before closing them; whether to ask the man who's just got on at the back to get off again; and whether to move off when the bus is now so full that passengers obscure the view to the nearside mirror. The driver makes a series of difficult decisions at nearly every stop on the journey between Croydon and Brixton.

In addition to these decisions, the driver has to make decisions to drive the bus! When to pull out, to overtake, to slow down, to stop or carry on at an amber light, to allow traffic to cross from a side road, to take special care of cyclists and pedestrians, some of whom dice with death as they weave in and out of the dense, slow-moving traffic. Driving a large vehicle with nearly a hundred people crammed tightly into it requires great skill; the responsibilities are onerous and the technical expertise is considerable.

SYSTEMS WITHIN SYSTEMS

The driver is the key person in this 'system' – the bus. The bus – as a socio-technical (people and technology) system – is interacting with all the other systems around it: most obviously the traffic systems of roads, lights, junctions, bus stops and schedules, Transport for London, the rail and tube systems and, of course, the people. The system of the bus meshes with all the different systems of which every passenger is a part, notably, at that time in the morning, the education system, shops, offices and the thousands of different workplaces to which people are travelling. Earlier buses would be carrying passengers going to work in the highly complex systems of hospitals and social care services.

The bus and all the other systems with which it interacts have their regulations, rules and procedures, but buses have just one purpose: they pick up passengers and take them to their destination. If the driver did not have that purpose foremost in mind at all times, the bus would stop. If safety inspectors were put on each bus to 'ensure' that the regulations were followed to the letter, the buses and the whole of London's rush hour would seize up. There would be fights and accidents, a massive increase in motor traffic and London would come to a halt. The driver is constantly making finely balanced decisions, weighing up purpose against safety and thereby keeping the system running. The bus's system has to flex and adapt, and intermesh with all the other systems in order that the massively complex overall system (London's rush hour) works.

The driver has a handbook called *The Big Red Book*. In the introduction, the managing director of 'surface transport' for London writes, 'If you're in doubt about how to handle a situation, think about how you would like to be treated and you will have the answer.' Throughout the handbook, drivers are asked to use their judgement to manage situations as best they can within an overall framework of guidance. The bus cannot be driven from outside, by managers or consultants, by inspectors or quality assurance experts, or by directives or rule-books. If the driver had to divert attention to satisfying the needs of the organisations that run and regulate the bus, the passengers would become secondary considerations and the whole system would grind to a halt. The system would also break down if the driver and passengers did not constantly negotiate the power they have. The driver does have the power to exclude and in many ways to make the passengers' journeys uncomfortable or inconvenient, but the passengers also have the power – individually and collectively – to disrupt the journey and to make the driver's job difficult.

At the end of the bus journey, perhaps 50 passengers get off the bus and cross the road to Brixton Underground Station, where hundreds more people are pouring down the escalators onto the trains. Sometimes the station gates are shut to reduce the pressure inside. People wait patiently, crammed against each other on the wide pavement. The gates open again and the waiting crowd flows down the steps into the station concourse where classical music imparts a calming and orderly ambiance, through the ticket barriers, down the escalators and onto the next available train.

There are, of course, occasions when everything does seize up: a traffic accident, a flood, a broken-down bus or truck, or the system is so overloaded that it just can't cope. All systems – and our whole lives as human beings – exist within a context, an environment. Everything affects everything else. When storms and floods disrupt transport and wreck people's homes and lives, although we might have contributed to the causes of such extreme weather, we can't control it but have to respond by flexing and adapting existing systems and creating new ones (such as dredging rivers and building flood defences) – all interconnected, all changing and adjusting as circumstances change.

The bus driver works in short episodes. Even in rush hour this is not a long bus journey. The bus turns at Brixton, and the return journey begins at Brixton Police Station. It is intense and demanding work. The driver manages. In the course of the journey, the bus picks up and drops several hundred passengers. While safety and the operating rules of the bus are extremely important and constant considerations, if the driver made them the *purpose* of the bus, the vehicle would never move, the passengers would not get to their destination, and the driver would fail in the 'core task'.

The complex interconnectedness of a bus journey in rush hour and the driver's role make it to some extent comparable with the job of managing social care. There are mass transport systems that are designed to be more isolated from – and thereby less enmeshed with – other systems around them. Notably, the Docklands Light Railway (DLR) has been designed so that it can be controlled remotely: there is no driver. There are far fewer decisions to make. It runs on rails; it stops and starts with automatic safety controls; the doors open and close; it is like a toy train set. The further removed government and policy makers are from the realities of the social care system, the more likely they are to aspire to run it like a toy train set. Social care just doesn't work like that.

ADDING LEADERSHIP TO MANAGEMENT

As complex and demanding as the bus driver's job is, the level of complexity, demand and challenge is as nothing compared with leading a social care service. The scale and dimensions of the jobs are in different leagues. While the driver may interact briefly with some passengers, the social care manager has a large staff team and many clients, and typically works with them over a period of years. The driver does have a responsibility to check that the bus is in good working order before taking it out of the garage, but the social care manager is responsible for all aspects of the building (in residential and day care work), office and plant (all the physical equipment, machinery and furniture) that go with the task. And, yes, above all, the *task* – the reason the service exists in the first place – is wider, taller, deeper and immensely more complex than driving a bus. Through its workforce (and to a lesser extent through its building, furniture and equipment) the care service forms a relationship with its clients, and it is through that relationship that the care is given.

A further significant difference is that the bus driver has been allotted a defined and achievable task and the resources to complete it, whereas the social care manager is set a task that is constantly changing and always impossible to fully achieve, and the available resources are never sufficient. Therefore, commonly used words and phrases such as 'ensure the delivery of personalised care packages, person-centred approaches, putting procedures in place to ensure quality, safety, dignity, etc.' reflect the toy train set mentality – a worrying misunderstanding of the negotiable, changeable and indefinable nature of the core task: good care.

Such a dynamic, complex and perpetually inadequate system requires not only competent management but courageous, creative and inspiring leadership. This book is principally about the leadership side of social care management: leading the task by diligent example; leading with the heart because the work is nothing if not emotional; and leading with artistic imagination by expressing your ideas and ideals in good care.

WHY I'VE WRITTEN THIS BOOK AND HOW, I HOPE, IT WILL HELP YOU TO LEAD GOOD CARE

By the time this book is published, I will have worked in social care for 50 years, ever since, after leaving school, I decided I wanted to experience the 'real world' rather than go to university. I joined up as a Community Service Volunteer and became a teaching assistant in a secondary school in Paddington while living as a resident in a probation hostel. By living at the hostel, sharing a room with three other young men who had been in prison, I experienced what it was like to be 'a resident' and thought how such a place could do a much better job by being run as a community where the residents took more responsibility for themselves, each other and the place.

After a variety of social care jobs, I began working as third-in-charge at a children's reception centre in 1968, going on to manage a large children's home called Frogmore in the 1970s. I took a full-time post-qualifying 'advanced' course at Bristol University in 1978 and then spent three years teaching social care and consulting to care homes. In the 1980s, I completed the Tavistock consultancy training (now called Consulting and leading in organisations: psychodynamic and systemic approaches); I managed a 120-bed local authority residential and day-care centre called Inglewood; and I took a Master's Degree in Public Policy at Bristol's School for Advanced Urban Studies. In the 1990s I headed a local charity (Richard Cusden Homes), wrote my first two books and became a Fellow of Michael Young's School for Social Entrepreneurs. From 2009 to 2013, I headed the Association of Care Managers campaigning for the professional development that this book is about. For more than 20 years I have worked as a consultant, writer, researcher, interim manager, tutor and teacher, inspector and – unpaid – been a campaigner, whistleblower and advocate. So, I've managed and worked with a wide variety of care services and I've written many hundreds of thousands of words on management in books, journals and magazines. In that time, I have witnessed the growth of a procedural, rule-bound, narrowly focused, do-as-you're-told, compliance culture that purports to provide stock solutions, but is contrary to social care values and simply doesn't work for the people for whom the services exist. This negative culture derives from a simplistic, anxiety-driven notion that care can be produced and delivered to order by 'putting systems in place', as if it were a commodity that can be remotely controlled like a toy train set. Care is not manufactured and delivered; care is essentially a relationship.

This book is a further attempt to set out and recommend a positive and hopeful vision of social care. My subtitle – the task, heart and art of managing social care – is both realistic and idealistic. The *task* requires serious, disciplined, hands-on, hard work. The *heart* signifies that this work is emotional and personal, and that care is a human relationship. And the *art* of managing care engages your skills, your imagination, your culture and creativity.

Having worked with hundreds of social care managers and been one myself, I feel that I know my readership quite well, but we are all different. This is certainly not an instruction book, nor is it a textbook. While the thinking and ideas are my own, they also come from other people but I have avoided crowding the book with references. I have adapted and built on other people's work to apply it to our social care leadership specialism. At the end of the book, you will find references to writing, people and organisations that have and still do help me to understand our work and may be helpful to you too.

I write at a time when we should be learning the lessons of a command-and-control culture, but we are in danger of replacing yet one more set of instructions with another. It was a do-as-you're-told, top-down, target driven culture that led to the atrocities of Stafford General Hospital and Winterbourne View. (Neither was an isolated case, just the most memorable and prominent scandals of abuse and neglect at the time of writing.) This 'delivery' culture was also characterised by the extraordinary selection and subsequent dominance of some of the most senior managers who recruited and protected each other and bullied their way to the top. Desperate to mend health and social care before the next election, politicians go on believing that it can be 'fixed', and the same old delivery culture believed that Jim could fix it for them. They recruited Sir James Wilson Vincent Savile, OBE, KCSG to 'manage' a secure psychiatric hospital where he abused patients. They gave him free rein to prey on hundreds of victims in many other care settings, while being honoured, protected, sponsored and used by the Establishment that he so assiduously courted. Like Savile, celebrities and members of the Establishment have raped and abused children and adults with impunity, while those who protested were ignored, silenced, threatened or punished and are only now being heard. The officials who colluded in concealing these crimes can still redeem themselves by exposing the truth about perpetrators in power. Abuse and exploitation are endemic in a top-down social care system that demeans, disempowers and damages the people who most need its help.

When you become a social care manager, you too may feel that in order to keep your job you will have to do as you're told, put up with what you know to be wrong, get high marks in your inspections, and convince your employers and regulators that you are in every way a thoroughly compliant employee. Indeed, this has been the problem with developing leadership in social care. For several reasons (some shared with the health service) social care has become a top-down, rule-orientated, highly competitive *and* bureaucratised service. Compliance and delivery are the watchwords; if you don't comply and you don't deliver, you are a failure. The truth is that this top-down system has been a disaster and managers have been left dealing with the perpetual and tragic failures of such a regime. Hitherto, the response to these failures has been to do more of the same, thereby only making matters worse.

This book takes a very different approach. As a leader, you will work out your own principles and set your own standards; you will take responsibility for your service and its task; you will encourage leadership in your team and assertiveness in the clients of your service. You will authorise yourself; in other words, you will embrace the leadership role you have been given and take the lead. My intention and hope is that in this book you will find analysis, understanding and inspiration for this difficult, essential and immensely rewarding task. Taking the lead means making decisions and sometimes being wrong, and then learning and moving on. It means taking the authority to lead and being given the authority to lead by your staff and your clients.

Writing any book, but especially writing a book on leadership, is an act of self-authorisation. To commit myself to writing, trusting my judgement and experience, knowing that it won't be perfect, exposing myself to criticism, daring to challenge established ways, is to believe in myself, hold true to principles and accept responsibility. Taking up the leadership of a social care service also requires self-authorisation: finding the authority from within yourself not only to manage your service, but to lead it. That's what this book is about.

INTRODUCTION
LEADING GOOD CARE
The Task, Heart and Art of Managing Social Care

For many readers, I hope this book will be surprising, challenging, thought provoking and amusing. Much writing, training and consultancy, and management of social care is about what you as the manager must do to comply with the demands of outsiders. If you are happy with doing as you are told, this is not the book for you. Here and in all of my consultancy work I encourage you to take a different direction, the direction that *you* set. It is about leading good care starting with the core task, using your emotions (heart) and your creativity and imagination (art). It is not a handbook and cannot give you the day-to-day practical guidance that a handbook should. (I strongly recommend that you obtain *The Social Care Manager's Handbook*, which is published annually by the National Skills Academy for Social Care, as an everyday guide to your job.) This book takes every aspect of the work to a deeper level, which may at first make you feel even more overwhelmed by the demands and complexity of your job; yet, when you understand the work at a deeper level, I hope you will see it more clearly and become optimistic about your ambitions for leading your social care service.

> No man is an Island, entire of itself; every man is a piece of the Continent, a part of the main; if a clod be washed away by the sea, Europe is the less as well as if a promontory were, as well as if a manor of thy friends or of thine own were; any man's death diminishes me, because I am involved in Mankind; and therefore never send to know for whom the bell tolls; it tolls for thee.
>
> (John Donne, *Devotions upon Emergent Occasions*, 1624)

We all live in a world of interlocking, interdependent systems. Everything is connected. This applies to our environment, to the human body, to families and households, to societies and to the organisations that we have created. To lead a good care service, we have to know what its purpose (core task) is, understand how it works and the context within which it works, how to build, maintain and improve a care system. A leader of good care works at the micro level and the macro level. We must also live and work in and with our world, learning how to respond and adapt, to be creative and survive.

CREATING A SYSTEMS MODEL

Leading Good Care – this book – is based on a systems model of your service…but one that you create in your mind. Each chapter explores a major aspect of your care system or building block of the model. My hand-drawn figures and diagrams are based on the model that I have in my mind when I'm facilitating learning groups or consulting to social care services. You can build your own model with your team or in action learning sets with other managers (see Appendix 1, 'Action Learning'), but I know that diagrams and models don't make sense to everyone and, if that is the case for you, please don't let them put you off. Concentrate on the stories of how four managers lead good care; reflect on your own experience, and create your own pictures in mind.

A systems model is only a model; it is a concept, an illustration; it's not the real thing. It is also a hypothesis set out as a means of exploring and understanding the reality. Like a map, a model is no substitute for being on the ground immersed in the experience, but it can help you to know where you are, how one area relates to another, to decide where you are going and by what route, and to reflect on your experience of being there. This model or concept is only one way of looking at, understanding and analysing social care services with the purpose of leading them more effectively. The model simulates, takes apart and illustrates the reality of your care service, which is a whole living organisation (organism) that in real life cannot be taken apart.

BUILDING SYSTEMS OF CARE FROM THE CORE TASK OUTWARDS

The central idea or proposition of the book is that good care is created always by starting with the core task. Whether we are considering a care home, home care agency, day centre, or a social services department, regulator, national charity or multinational care corporation, we will make it work properly for the people who use it only if we start with them and the job they need doing.

This, of course, is how organised social care started: by people getting together to meet a social need that could not be adequately met by family, partner, neighbours or friends. However, even in a small organisation, the core task can get undermined, sidelined or forgotten when the conscious and unconscious anti-task forces (that are always present in organisations) take over from leadership.

STORIES OF MANAGERS TAKING THE LEAD

At each stage of creating the model, in each chapter of the book, stories will be told of four managers taking the lead in their service: Gita, leading a care home for older people; Gill, leading a therapeutic community for adults who have learning disabilities; Gloria, leading a home care cooperative, and Geoff, leading a local multi-purpose resource centre. Because legislation, regulation and guidance are in constant flux, and because this book is focused on the principles and practice of leading good care rather than on the external and superficial demands that often only undermine good care, few references are made to specific legislation or regulation. (You will find that the National Skills Academy for Social Care's *The Social Care Manager's Handbook* will be your first resource when it comes to current legislation and guidance.) So, for example, we know regulation and inspection is a major issue for all managers but the rules and requirements change all the time, and this book is not about being compliant with regulations and doing as you are told; it is about leading with your own standards and principles. As a leader of good care, you must take the initiative, as do the managers in the developing stories that are used as examples. While being based on real people and organisations, these stories are fictitious, simplified versions of real events. Again, you must use your imagination (as with any story) to transpose them to your real situation and experience, to tell and reflect on your own stories, to use, build on and learn from your own experience.

THE THEORETICAL BASE

You will find that there are very few references to other books. I have drawn on theory, tested and retested and adapted in nearly 50 years' practice, that I have been absorbing all my working life. I have been strongly influenced by the psychosocial systems thinking of the Tavistock Institute and Clinic (where I did my consultancy training), by continuing learning from OPUS (Organisation for Promoting Understanding of Society), and by several other societies and organisations such as Vanguard Consulting

(John Seddon). You will find a list of books and other resources at the end. So there is no literature review, and this is not an academic book. However, I believe the theory to be sound in practice, which is what is most important to me and to you as practitioners.

WAYS OF USING THE BOOK

At the end of most chapters there are suggestions for thinking, discussion and activities related to the subject of the chapter for you to use on your own or in learning groups with other managers.

The stories (case studies) may be useful as starting points for discussion, but do share, tell and reflect on your own experience and your own feelings. Reading the stories may give you access to your stories.

I have structured the book in a logical fashion – context, task, feelings, boundaries, managing, making wider changes and leading change. You don't have to read it from start to finish. You could start at the end and work backwards, or in the middle and work from there both ways. Anticipating that not everyone reads a book from the beginning, I have tried to include in each chapter some explanation about what has gone before, and that means there is some repetition. So, each of the 'building blocks' of the model is repeated frequently: core task, boundary and what is 'beneath the surface' are always issues wherever you are in your endeavour of leading good care.

THE SOCIAL CARE MANAGER'S PROFESSIONAL DEVELOPMENT AND SELF-AUTHORISATION

It's now a long time (16 years) since I wrote my last proper book about managing social care (*Managing Residential Care*, Routledge, 1998). In that book, I wrote that managers were the key to improvement: '…if we take the opportunity, we will lead a change that will transform, enrich and elevate our whole society'. We (social care managers) still have the opportunity to take the authority to change our services. Only we can do it, and there are managers who are leading great changes now. I write what I believe in and hope for, and I don't expect everyone to agree with me, but I will go on trying to persuade.

For a while now, I have been a leading member of the steering group of the National Skills Academy for Social Care Registered Managers' Programme. We are launching an important change in social care that is led by you, and this book is part of that initiative. That is not to claim that my fellow steering group members will all agree with this book; indeed, I can guarantee that several will disagree with it! But I hope that the book is sufficiently influential to make a significant difference to the way social care is led, managed, and thereby improved, and to the way in which managers learn and are qualified to do their (your) essential and exciting jobs. I very strongly urge you to join up with other managers locally and nationally, join the National Skills Academy's registered managers' development programme and receive as part of your membership *The Social Care Manager's Handbook*. In the handbook, you will find all the day-to-day, essential information (that is not in this book) to enable you to keep your service running well, while you use this book to think, imagine, discuss and develop as a leading professional, authorising yourself to change social care fundamentally and for the better.

STORIES OF LEADING GOOD CARE

Throughout the book there are stories of the task, heart and art of good care featuring four managers leading four different care services, and some of the people who are using the services. These examples are fictitious but based on real people, real services and real events that I have been involved with as a care worker, manager, consultant and inspector. I use them to illustrate the real possibilities of providing consistently good care when managers grasp and are given the authority to lead. All four managers are highly effective, but not perfect. Good care is found, expressed and provided through human relationships and is therefore never perfect. Good enough will do.

Because I've used the managers' stories to provide examples of how aspects of management and leadership play out in practice, they are not in time sequence, so a story in a later chapter may refer to something that happens before the story of the same manager in an earlier chapter.

The stories provide case studies for discussion, but I hope they will also stimulate you to share your own real experiences with other managers. Just as the greater part of good care is in relationships, in lived experience, so is the greater part of professional development in using your own and others' real experience as the basis for all learning.

The legislative context of social care frequently changes and I have been careful not to refer to specific legislation, policies, guidance and procedures. (Again, *The Social Care Manager's Handbook* is an excellent current guide to the immediate practicalities of managing.) The stories here are in a sense timeless, because they portray managers and clients engaged in issues and events that will always be with us as part of social care in its wider context. When a social care service works well for people, it is because it works with and is integrated with its neighbourhood and other services. Such integration is best achieved at a local level by people taking the initiative to work together. When collaboration and integration happen, it is always led by the managers of the services, and the stories here illustrate how that comes about even when statutory social care and health services are slow to join in. Much is made of the divisive effects of competition in a mixed economy of care (for profit, not for profit and statutory), but in these examples collaboration is good for clients and therefore literally pays off for all providers.

All these services are based in and around a city I call **Careborough**, which is the largest conurbation in the county and local authority of **Careshire**. So, the setting for the stories is both urban and rural.

The people and places in the stories

Gita manages **The Limes**, a 60-bedded care home for older people on the outskirts of the city. It has four care households, each of them managed by a team leader. The home is owned by a multinational private provider, which has a good reputation but has, in the opinion of its new managing director **Sarah**, become stale and complacent, and urgent change is needed. Sarah has appointed Gita to reform and renew the care, starting with The Limes, but with the objective of leading change in the whole company. **Ellen** is a housekeeper for one of the households at The Limes but also does some care work, and acts as a keyworker. **Mrs Smith**, after using two of the other services, takes up residence at The Limes. **Grace** is the care worker who takes over from Ellen as Mrs Smith's keyworker.

Gill manages **The Willows**, an eight-bedded care home for adults with learning disabilities, part of a medium-sized regional voluntary organisation. The home is in a village, five miles from Careborough. Gill leads a team of support workers and a housekeeper. The home operates as a small therapeutic community. **Martha** and **Edwin** are residents, and **Karl** is a member of staff.

Gloria leads **4Cs** (the City and County Care Company), a home care cooperative social enterprise with a very wide variety of clients, including **Mrs Smith** and, later, **Martha**. The support workers (who are also shareholders) work in small groups close to their own homes. They organise their own work in neighbourhood teams. The larger teams work in the city, where the majority of clients live. Here the teams of support workers live within walking or cycling distance, or they use the bus. Outside the town, the same principle applies – local self-managing teams living near to their clients, although some do need to use cars.

Geoff is the director of **The Hub**, a multi-purpose resource centre run by a consortium of local voluntary organisations and supported by the local authority. The management committee is made up of members (including users) from each of the voluntary organisations that runs services and activities at the centre. The Hub was one of Careshire's care homes, until they closed it and leased it to a housing association which converted the building into extra-care and sheltered housing (on the upper floors) and The Hub resource centre on the ground floor.

Mrs Smith, who is in her 80s, uses three services (4Cs, The Hub and The Limes) and has a connection through Edwin with The Willows.

Edwin is in his early 40s. He lives at The Willows and works at The Hub. He has a brief, one-sided relationship with Martha and a long-term relationship with Jean.

Martha is in her early 20s. She lived at The Willows for several months and then had to leave. She moved to a flat at The Hub (managed by a local housing association) and is supported by 4Cs. Martha has an exceptional singing voice and can play the piano by ear, so her support worker has linked her up with The Limes where she runs a very enthusiastic singing group on Thursday mornings.

Jean is in her early 30s. Edwin is her boyfriend. She attends various events and clubs at The Hub. She is a helper at the lunch club that Mrs Smith attends and she's a member of The Hub Caps, who are a group of volunteers.

Careshire Social Care Managers' Network

Gita, Gill, Gloria and Geoff are founding members of a social care managers' network. There are more than 30 members of the network who support and learn from each other, but not everyone can come to every meeting. This network has also set up action learning sets (see Appendix 1), independent supervision and a mentoring scheme, and is on the way to becoming **The Careshire Social Care Partnership**, with all the services collaborating to provide comprehensive social care in the locality.

1

CONTEXT AND INTEGRATION

Your service is an integral part of its neighbourhood, community and locality, and it also exists in the wider social, cultural, political and economic context. It has the potential to both change and be changed by the context within which it works. It can be a well-known, well-used and much appreciated local resource. Alternatively, while being geographically located in a community, it can seem remote and isolated from that community and almost exclusively controlled by and responsible to external organisations.

YOUR CARE SERVICE IN ITS CONTEXT

Most social care services in Britain serve the area in which they are located. There are exceptions – regional or national services – but they are few and far between almost by definition. However, all social care operates within the wider social, cultural, political and economic context. Indeed, as with all other aspects of 21st century life, care services are strongly influenced by global events and trends, by wars and famines, and by the vicissitudes of multinational corporations…and, yes, by weather, global warming, energy and food production.

Imagine the satellite picture: at first seeing your service on one side of the world, then zooming in to see it in the continent, the country, the region, city or county, the neighbourhood, the street and the building itself. At all these levels of magnification, you would see the context of your service.

FIGURE 1.1 YOUR CARE SERVICE IN ITS CONTEXT

While much of this book will encourage you to focus on leading your service for your clients in your neighbourhood, you will not do that effectively without seeing your service's place and connections with its environment in the widest possible sense. An awareness of what's going on in the world, of national and local politics, and an understanding of demographic trends as well as the current economic situation and forecasts will all help you to manage your service.

Urban – and, increasingly, rural – care services are likely to have multiracial and multicultural staff teams, and this can be of great advantage, but only if you as manager make good use of the diversity of your team, turning what may at first appear to be a disadvantage into an opportunity. The composition of staff teams and the labour market is very strongly influenced by world events and economic trends, and it would be as unwise and unjust to discriminate against any of your staff team as it would be to reject clients on grounds of race, culture or religion.

CARE SERVICES THAT ARE INTEGRAL
TO THEIR ENVIRONMENT

Gita, Gill, Gloria and Geoff, our four managers, all work in the county of Careshire. They all know each other and their different services work together. Often they have clients in common. They come from different backgrounds: Gita is from India, Gill from Cornwall, Gloria from Nigeria and Geoff from Newcastle. Their staff come from all over the world although the majority were born in the UK, and the same goes for their clients. This reflects the population of Careshire as a whole.

World events, international and national politics and policies, immigration and employment policies, education and training, the domestic economy and social care legislation and policy – to name just a few aspects of the wider social care environment – all have their short-, medium- and long-term effects on the services that our four managers lead. The local authority (Careshire Council), the city's supermarkets, bus services and the weather are also strongly influential. Indeed, everything has some effect. The four services are part of their environment.

NO SOCIAL CARE SERVICE IS
'AN ISLAND ENTIRE OF ITSELF'

It would, of course, be absurd for a home care service not to be working 'in the community' but many such services are not 'part of the community'. While some care homes are very much part of their locality, others are isolated from the world around them. As with any organisation under pressure, but more so, care homes can become like fortified castles, almost to the point where the appearance of a moat and a drawbridge wouldn't come as a surprise! Attacked and under pressure from outside, and starved of resources on the inside, the collective state of mind is often referred to as the siege mentality. There are times when an organisation needs a temporary period of retreat and introspection, when it is necessary to withdraw and protect itself while some rebuilding is done, but this must not become a permanent state; otherwise it will lead to stagnation and extinction (see 'Reinstating a broken boundary' in Chapter 4).

4CS HOME CARE SERVICE

Gloria came to the UK from Nigeria with her husband, soon to be followed by her young family, in the 1980s. Although she had degrees in English and Economics, she worked as a home help for the local authority until the service was 'outsourced' to independent providers, a mixture of private and voluntary, for-profit and not-for-profit organisations. Gloria loved the work; the flexible hours suited her and she was very good at it. She became an area manager for one of the private companies but wasn't happy with an ethos that exploited (underpaid and overworked) its workers in order to secure council contracts and generate a large profit. Gloria had kept contact with many of her old colleagues, some of whom were facing the same problems with their employers and were very dissatisfied with the care they were providing. Together they formed a new employee-owned company that became 4Cs (City and County Care Cooperative).

4Cs is now one of the main providers of home care (and many other related services) in Careshire and Careborough. It is well known and trusted and, as an integral part of the wider care system and the community, 4Cs works and has worked with most of the other local social care providers and their clients, Gita's, Gill's and Geoff's services amongst them.

NEIGHBOURHOOD, COMMUNITY, LOCALITY

Most of your clients and staff are likely to live or to have previously lived within a few miles of your administrative centre (the building in which or from which you operate). A few care homes that provide very specialised care draw on a national or regional clientele but, even then, most of the staff will be local and the people who live there are likely to wish to make connections and use facilities within the local community.

If your staff live locally (which is not always possible for everyone), they will have local connections – with schools, churches and other places of worship, pubs and clubs, shops, sports, places of entertainment, and with their own neighbours. These are all potentially valuable connections, and staff should be encouraged both to bring their community to work in some ways and to integrate the care home, day care centre or office base with the community(ies) they know.

THE LIMES AS A LOCAL RESOURCE

Although The Limes, Gita's care home, is part of a large national company (itself a subsidiary of a multinational company), it is seen by the residents and their relatives, and the staff and neighbourhood as a local resource. Gita is always at pains to play down the national company identity and to play up the home's place in and contribution to the community. Whenever there is an opportunity to get involved in local events and to open the resources of the home to locals, Gita takes it.

She also encourages the staff to be involved in their children's schools, local clubs and societies, pubs, churches and other faith groups, sports and cultural events. She likes staff to bring the neighbourhood into The Limes and to take The Limes out to the neighbourhood.

Various groups meet at The Limes; some, like the relatives' and friends' group, have close connections with the residents and their care; and some, like the stamp collectors, simply use a downstairs room once a month and open their membership to any residents who like to come...and one does. There are coffee mornings and an afternoon art class. And the local gardening club, which has its main meetings at The Hub, maintains the beautiful gardens at The Limes, including a productive kitchen garden with a polytunnel, and holds its annual show there. The connections with churches are strong, and people from the nearby Sikh temple bring food every weekend and have a small party for all who wish to come. There is always something going on at The Limes so the residents see many people from outside coming and going, and they feel a part of their neighbourhood.

Gita has had many discussions with the company that owns The Limes to persuade them that this feeling of local involvement and 'ownership' is beneficial to the company as well as supporting the best care of residents. She argues that if the branding of the company is too prominent, it begins to look as if anything that The Limes provides – even the care which is its core task – is simply done to swell the profits of shareholders, and as soon as that perception takes hold, the home and its task lose credibility and commitment. In addition, Gita points out that if you highlight the corporate ownership and something awful happens in another home under the same ownership, people will quickly associate the company – and therefore The Limes – with poor practice, neglect or abuse.

Meanwhile, Careshire (the local authority) likes to claim that the use of care homes as local resources is all part of their drive for 'personalisation' through 'asset-based community development' in their 'vision of a connected population where everyone has the opportunity to prosper, be healthy and happy'. Hurrah! Included in their own contract compliance assessment of care homes is the extent to which they are serving a wider community than just their residents. Another way of putting this would be, as the council cuts their services, people are thrown back on getting support from wherever they can.

ECONOMIC CONTEXT

Care services are important local sources of employment and have significant buying power when it comes to food and other supplies. As a manager, it will be good policy in the long run (if possibly a little more expensive in simple money terms) to use local suppliers even though your company may be attempting to make you buy from 'central' but distant suppliers (see 'The core task is the whole task' in Chapter 2).

It is common for the medium and large corporate providers of care to centralise their purchase of supplies, employing special head office staff to negotiate deals that reduce the unit price. However, if this job becomes part of the care home, for example, and the housekeeping manager in the home takes responsibility for it, you can take advantage of buying from local suppliers. Because, in care homes, supplies and other provisions – especially food – are such an important part of the life and work of the place, it's important to bring control of them inside the home. This opens up participation to the whole care community and should be linked with how the whole budget is managed. Provider organisations may also consider that if buying provisions, maintenance…everything…from within the home, there is no need to staff a specialist purchasing team at the head office, and the result may be a considerable saving overall while making budgeting and buying a therapeutic activity and an integral part of the life of the home.

So, your service is a little 'economy' of its own with a turnover of hundreds of thousands – sometimes millions – of pounds. A large care home in a village is likely to be amongst the biggest local employers. The annual income could be more than £4m, with a wage bill of more than half that. Local shops and businesses will depend on the trade that they get from the home and the staff. Housing will be affected by the dominance of such a large employer. To what extent the home is seen as a positive influence or as dominant but negative will depend very much on how much the provider connects and engages with the village or neighbourhood. Do people see it as 'their' care home? Are they proud of it? Is it connected with the school, church and pub?

The wages and salaries of your staff are influenced by a combination of factors: the minimum wage; the local authority fees and the ratio of self-funders to those who are state-funded; local wage levels and competition for recruitment; the demand for care and the occupancy rates at the home; the dividend, profit or surplus that your proprietor organisation intends to make; interest rates; the fluctuating prices of goods and services; and so on. The same goes for all other care services. Too many local authorities have cut and cut again the money they will pay for people who are supported in their own homes. The timing of visits has been reduced so that some people receive 15-minute visits and some care staff are not paid for the time they take to get from one client to another. The councils claim that their need to pare down visits and raise eligibility criteria is driven by cuts in the money they receive from government. While this is true, it is not the whole explanation and should not be used as an excuse for colluding with reducing care for people who are in need or for underfunding care. In the same way, you too cannot simply wring your hands and do nothing while staff are underpaid and your clients are shabbily treated. As a leader, you must take a stand and still do your best with reduced resources.

THE HUB: AT THE CENTRE OF COMMUNITY ACTION AND ACTIVITY

The Hub was set up by Careshire social services, the Careshire Housing Association and a consortium of local voluntary organisations. It had been a large local authority care home until the county council decided to close it and sell the land for development. An alternative plan was put forward – and eventually accepted – to turn the building into a multi-use community resource centre to include flats for older and disabled people with high support needs.

The Hub was by name and design at the centre of its locality and neighbourhood, but it would take Geoff's skilled coordination and leadership to get all the different user groups and organisations to put aside their rivalries, power struggles and antagonisms, and concentrate on the core task: to serve the social needs and development of the local community. While it was a deliberately broad remit encompassing care, recreation and culture, it did not include the enrichment, aggrandisement and empire building that some of the organisations involved were prone to.

The Hub could so easily have been dominated by the established and professionally managed organisations that were involved from the beginning, but were not the people or groups that fought to prevent a public resource from being sold off to the highest bidder. These larger organisations' way of operating was similar to the local authority's and the housing association's. When it came to tendering for and contracting to supply services, they had a great advantage over the small and amateur alliances which might want to start an activity or support group but lacked the cash and expertise to apply for public funds. The established organisations tended to forget that they too started small, without funds or staff but with an idea that they wanted to make a reality.

The management board of The Hub was numerous and unwieldy. All organisations had to have a user representative on the board, but it was dominated by the voluntary organisation professionals, the housing association and the council. Fortunately, Geoff, who attended all board meetings as the director, had a strong and independent chairperson who stood up for the small organisations and the users. She was a user herself. She and the other officers (treasurer and secretary) were elected at the AGM each year where all users of The Hub had a vote.

Geoff observed that the economic and social context of The Hub was changing. Cuts to local government funding were in turn cutting into the funding of the established non-government organisations that had been used to take over the functions of the local authority. Increasingly people would have to organise themselves to meet needs. The established voluntary organisations were competing with each other for resources and Geoff could see that the time would come when the bureaucratic model of these charities (which had been successful for so long) would become unsustainable, outdated and inept. The future of social care, in Geoff's view, was in very local action, and that was his vision for The Hub. Soon there would be more very elderly people needing support than there were younger retired people to provide it. New groups of immigrants were organising care for their own communities, and their self-help initiatives were an example to others, but also created some friction and envy. Meanwhile the council provided care only for those in dire need and, for all the well-paid talk about personalisation and prevention, there was little evidence of either on the ground, and individual budgets were being trimmed back, thus further undermining personalisation.

Like so many other democratic institutions, from the county council to the government, The Hub could have lost connection with the very community it was set up to serve as it became professionalised, bureaucratised and proceduralised. So, at the heart of Geoff's leadership role was keeping the place and all its activities connected with the people of the local community rather than with the organisations that claimed to represent their interests. The pressures to conform with external organisational expectations were great and were much the same as the pressures on Gloria, Gita and Gill. Like them, Geoff had to steer a fine line between working with the established organisations that funded and to a large extent controlled The Hub, and supporting and encouraging grass-roots activism to meet immediate and urgent needs.

SOCIAL, CULTURAL AND POLITICAL CONTEXT

It will be immediately evident that it is not possible to separate the economic context from the social, cultural and political context. Yes, they all affect each other. They not only affect and interact with each other, they determine each other. For example, the concept of social class is rarely at the centre of everyday discussion, yet it has great influence on all aspects of modern life and work. We are inclined to forget, deny or ignore class. The dividing lines between classes were never very clear but they are even less clear now than they have ever been. Many working-class children of the postwar 'baby boomer' generation (my generation) went to university or college and became by dint of education, qualifications, job, income and housing very much middle class.

Care work is generally poorly paid and does not require an academic qualification for entry. However, a care worker may gain experience and promotion, take professional training and get qualifications, and be appointed as manager of a care service. Somewhere along this career path, this person moves from a combination of working-class characteristics to a new combination of middle-class attributes. Another manager may have started in the same job at the same time but was middle class all along. Yet another may value their working-class roots and culture to such an extent that they hang on to their class identity even when they have moved into a middle-class job. None of these is 'right' or 'wrong' in itself, but all aspects of your identity as a manager and leader are significant, and establishing your honesty and authenticity (the real you) is essential if you expect people to relate to you as a person and follow your lead.

The same issues of class are there for your clients. Some care homes, for example, are very middle class. They are likely to have more self-funders (residents who have no state funding), and the decor and furnishing may be like a smart hotel. Indeed, going by the style and design of most modern care homes, the 'hotel model' seems to be the aim, and this is especially true as self-funders outnumber state-subsidised residents. Some working-class residents may find such a place too fancy for them and yearn for somewhere more homely, informal and sociable. Bingo might appeal more than bridge. And some highly educated and cultured residents (of any class) may also find one of these 'care hotels' oppressively genteel and dull.

As a manager of social care, you need to be aware of your own tastes and prejudices, and of your own identity. Knowing an area, other countries, customs, religions, cultures and languages, some history and politics, and being genuinely interested in people will help you to create a service that appeals to a wide variety of people, and that can change and adapt to meets their care needs (the core task). And it is important – for you, your staff and your clients – that you express and maintain your own culture and identity, whatever they are (see 'Integrity and authenticity' in Chapter 7).

Religion and politics have strong influences on our care services. For example, if you run a care service in Northern Ireland, you and your clients will be surrounded and infused with religion and politics. To pretend otherwise would be folly. All over Britain, various religions and a wide variety of political opinions are likely to exist, wherever you are, and are a part of everyone's lives.

YOUR CARE SERVICE IN AN INTERNATIONAL CONTEXT

Many care services are staffed by people who have come from other parts of the world to work, and many of them have left families and dependants behind. They share their pay; they send money home. They may be relatively highly educated and qualified but have come to support their families by taking any job that they can, often at or near the minimum wage. They are in a vulnerable position as employees because the loss of the job, even the loss of overtime or a reduction in standard hours, may hurt them even more than colleagues permanently based in the UK. They are also subject to widespread prejudice that sees them as interlopers, perhaps illegal immigrants, as takers rather than givers; yet, in reality, their vulnerability is often cruelly exploited. They may feel that they can afford neither to trust their employers nor offend them by raising any issue whether it be their conditions of employment or shortcomings in care. Sometimes they are doing two or more jobs and living in poor housing. They need to save money for occasional trips home. News of natural disasters and political upheavals at home may have devastating effects on them.

As a manager, you should learn about the background of all your staff, whose diversity will be an asset and who, with very few exceptions, will repay your concern for them handsomely in loyalty and commitment.

THE WILLOWS: A THERAPEUTIC COMMUNITY WITHIN ITS NEIGHBOURHOOD

Before Gill became manager of The Willows, it was known locally as 'the home'. There was little interaction between the residents of The Willows and the people living either side of the building, let alone with those living in the streets around. The residents came and went, often in the home's minibus or in 'transport' (meaning council or hospital vehicles). The staff just worked there: they turned up in their cars, did their 'shift', and left to go back to their homes to live their lives elsewhere. Small as it was – just eight residents – The Willows then was an institution, a place of work and a minor blot on the landscape for the neighbours.

When Gill arrived, she led a change. While staff were at work, she expected them to share their lives with the residents. She understood that The Willows and its residents were isolated from the surrounding neighbourhood and that the home couldn't work properly for residents until it became part of the neighbourhood. She thought about the whole system and how the staff were complicit in this isolation.

She discouraged those who drove their cars to work from parking them at the front of the house. If they had to come to work by car (and some did have to), she wanted them to park in the street and walk in. None of the residents had a car but parking space was taking up most of the front garden. Gill said that three (instead of eight) parking spaces were sufficient: one for the large car that was the house vehicle, and two for visitors. Gill felt that the cars gave several wrong messages. One was dividing residents from staff and then staff from the neighbourhood of which The Willows should be part. Another message was aesthetic and ecological; cars are neither attractive nor green and don't belong in a garden. Yet another was more difficult to nail down but had something to do with the freedom – or power – of the staff to come and go as they pleased without effort or dependence on other people. Driving was an expression of power and a type of self-sufficiency that seemed antithetical to the principles of a therapeutic community.

Some staff failed at first to see the point of Gill's opposition to their parking cars at the front, but it led into many other discussions and explorations of the meaning of community and neighbourliness. Gradually all the staff learned to walk into work, to say hello to neighbours, to catch buses with the residents, and to get to know the streets and the people living around The Willows. The residents also began to see the people around them, and got noticed and engaged with as individuals in return, rather than just looked at out of curiosity and some anxiety as the strange people from 'the home'.

Instead of being a car park, the front garden was a mass of colour and interest all year round. Everyone at The Willows was proud of the front garden and it was often a topic of conversation with passing neighbours. In the comparatively large back garden there was a good-sized vegetable patch and a greenhouse as well as a lawn, patio and barbecue. And there was a chicken run with six brown hens.

The change that Gill led from a conventional residential 'home' or institution to a therapeutic community, from isolation to integration, took some time. The concept of a 'home' for people with learning disabilities was easy for neighbours to understand...and not to be involved with. You were just unlucky if you found yourself living next door to such a home, and it certainly reduced the value of your property. But if neighbours had first been asked if they would prefer to live near to a 'therapeutic community', the answers would probably have been no. Yet the effect of The Willows becoming a therapeutic community was to increase the sense and value of community in the whole neighbourhood. The relationship was mutually beneficial: The Willows did a lot for the neighbourhood and the neighbourhood did a lot for The Willows.

YOUR SERVICE AS A 'SOCIAL ECOLOGY' IN A WORLD ECOLOGY

If we experience and position ourselves and act as beings in a system within an infinite number of systems which make up a whole world system, which is again only a system within another infinite number of systems, we can see a social care service as a part of a world ecology. The economic development of South America, Africa and India does have a bearing on our care services. The depletion of the world's resources, world trade, climate change, revolutions and wars, migration and food production, water and fossil fuels, are perpetually changing the ecology not only of countries and continents but of the tiny part of the whole world system that we work in. Like it or not, we are connected. We influence and are influenced. We cannot escape our ecology.

We can use this as an analogy – our care service as a 'therapeutic social ecology' – and acknowledge (know) it as an actuality. As I write now, widespread and catastrophic flooding is devastating southern England. Who is to blame? God? The solar system? The government? The Environment Agency? Local authorities? Builders and planners? The multinationals? The supermarkets? Farmers? Householders? The new care home in the Thames catchment area that turned a garden into a car park? The home care service that has its underpaid staff hurrying around to appointments in clapped out old cars that they cannot afford to maintain? The local authority that beats down the price of home care so only the worst employers win the contract? Or was it the competitive greed of the international banks that set off the world financial crisis? Or was it 9/11? And so on.

Your service is itself a micro-ecology. While it is part of the world ecology, it – and you – have decisions and choices to make, directions to take. How closely will you engage with the community around you? To what extent will your service be controlled and directed from outside and how much from inside? Is your service working as a system that can respond to the needs it was set up to meet, or is it working to meet the needs and demands of external organisations? These are some of the questions that arise when you start thinking about the service you lead in its wider context.

SUGGESTIONS FOR DISCUSSION AND ACTIVITY
Your care service's place in the world

- Get a wall map of the world and mark all the places that staff and clients come from or have family connections with.

- Use this in a team meeting.

- Ask people to talk about their origins to the rest of the group. Don't exclude local connections.

- Ask people to bring pictures or mementos of home – whatever that means to them.

Your care service's connection with current affairs and issues

- Talk about political, economic, religious and spiritual, ecological…any…issues that affect the service, as they come up in the news. Take newspaper cuttings (or print internet news pages) and use them to stimulate discussion.

- On a large piece of paper or using a whiteboard, putting your service in the centre, plot all the outside influences there are on the service. Be specific; try to avoid generalisations.

Your care service's connections with its neighbourhood and community

- Do you know the neighbours?

- Who else do you know in the street/area/village?

- Who comes in?

- What events do you go to?

- What shops, pubs, churches and other places of worship, places of entertainment and businesses do you use?

- What are your connections with local schools and colleges?

Your care service's connection with other services and organisations?

Use the stories in this chapter as vignettes to stimulate thought and team discussions, for example:

- car parking

- the neighbours

- use of the garden

- central or local purchasing

- staying close to the community

- what is a therapeutic community?

2

CARE, THE CORE TASK

Your service has **one core purpose** or task – providing good care for the people who use it. This means that you lead an organisation or team with that core purpose in mind at every moment. Judge everything you do as manager by its relevance to this task and, if it's not relevant, don't do it.

The core or primary task of a care service is usually explicit in its description. A 'care home' provides care and home: a place to live which becomes a home and where staff are employed to look after or care for those aspects of life (including social and emotional) that the individual can no longer manage independently. A 'day care centre' provides a lower level of care for a shorter period, but possibly to a wider range of users, during the day. And 'home care' or 'domiciliary care' provides a wide range of care in the person's own home.

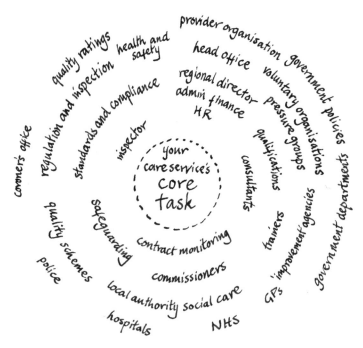

FIGURE 2.1 YOUR CARE SERVICE'S CORE TASK

However, while as manager you need to be clear about such a straightforwardly defined core task, your employers, the company or voluntary organisation you work for, the local authority, your regulator and quality assurance assessors – even your trainers and consultants – may not be clear about their core task and its relationship to your core task. Currently, all these outside bodies tend to assume that your task and the task of your service is to fulfil their own expectations of what you should be doing to meet their demands. This means that the tasks of care services can become muddled and ill defined, and pull you in different directions.

THE CORRUPTION OF THE CORE TASK

An employer like Castlebeck (the company that owned and ran Winterbourne View), while purporting to put the care of its clients above all other considerations, is in the care business with the sole object of making money for its owners. Castlebeck itself was jointly owned by Lydian Capital Partners, an investment 'club' that included John Magnier and JP McManus, and by the banks that, in 2006, funded the purchase of Castlebeck for £255m. The company employed 2100 people, provided 'care' for 580 people at 56 locations, and charged the taxpayer £3,500 a week for the appalling 'treatment' of each patient. To its owners, Castlebeck was no different from a racehorse, football club, gold mine, arms manufacturer or bank. What mattered was its short-term profitability. And when abuse and torture were exposed at Winterbourne View by the BBC *Panorama* programme in May 2011, all the outside bodies which, in different ways, had oversight of and responsibility for the care of the people living there, reacted by imposing more of the measures and practices that had already failed to protect the residents of Winterbourne View. Instead of examining their own core tasks in relation to care providers, they reinforced systems of regulation and review that had already failed so tragically.

Even voluntary organisations may be tempted to imitate their commercial equivalents at the expense of their founding principles. In the name of survival, 'competition' and growth, they too take their eyes off the core task. The 'business', the chief executive's pay, 'branding', expansion, aggrandisement and the balance sheet can combine to become the main driving forces in a charity's existence. The local branches are mere outposts of the central organisation, feeding its hunger for national status and influence, advertising and expansion. Fundraising itself can take over as the core task of a charity, even to the point where it raises funds to finance television adverts to raise more funds.

Whether operating for profit or not, the care providers who succeed in the long run are the ones that understand that their financial health depends on how well they accomplish the core task of care. Their income, occupancy rates, reputation and standing as care providers are all determined by how well they provide care.

RESTORING THE CORE TASK AT THE LIMES

Gita's predecessor at The Limes had kept the home full. The company that owned and ran The Limes had built in incentives for managers and some other senior staff (including the people who sold 'beds' on commission). This had meant that there were rarely vacancies, but some residents were accepted even when the home could not provide the level of care that people needed. This in turn led to dissatisfied staff leaving, low morale and a general cynicism about the manager and the company.

A new managing director (Sarah) was appointed and she understood the problem. It was she who looked for a manager who could reverse this downward spiral and, she hoped, give a new direction to the company and prove that total dedication to the core task worked on the ground.

Gita took the job on the understanding that she would have a free hand to make the necessary changes. The managing director herself was up against the opposition of those in the company who believed that staff were mainly motivated by financial incentives and were no different from the company's shareholders in that respect. They argued that the company was successful and making a good profit, and generally had a good reputation for care, and The Limes was 'fully compliant' with the regulator's standards, so why change it?

Both Sarah and Gita knew that the care was not good enough, that sooner or later this would be exposed and, with sufficient adverse publicity, the company, its profits and its share price could collapse. The changes that Gita had been appointed to lead would restore the core task – good care for the residents – to its central position, and thereby, they argued, assure the company of honest, well-deserved, long-term profitability. Gita considered herself to be well paid and was not interested in earning bonuses for ignoring her own professional standards.

Many local authority adult care services are also in danger of losing sight of their core task because their main role has been relegated to commissioning, assessing and arranging care which is provided by third parties. They have less money with which to buy care but, because they have failed to provide support when it is first needed, they now have more people needing urgent care. They have therefore become rationers or gatekeepers rather than providers, concentrating on reducing cost not increasing value, and on preventing access to care rather than giving support to prevent high-cost emergency treatment being required. The opportunities for direct social care work with clients in local authorities are rare, because the 'social services' now see their task as assessing need rather than meeting it, and then passing on the work to service providers. There is precious little service in 'social services'. The local authority buys care from its contractors in a range of pre-packaged portions (which may include 15-minute 'slots') designed through a cut-price commissioning process that is dishonestly claimed to be 'person-centred' and 'personalised'.

STANDARDS, QUALITY AND COMPLIANCE

Standards and 'quality' are not core tasks. While it is essential that there are national standards and regulations so that people who use your service have legal protection from neglect and abuse, and can demand that care is up to standard, 'compliance' with such standards and regulations can become an end in itself, because a service that is not compliant with regulations is unlikely to survive for long. However, if the core task becomes achieving 'compliance' for survival, your true core task of good care will not be achieved, because 'compliance' is not the same as good care.

Compliance with externally set standards and quality benchmarks corrupts the core task. The central activity of the organisation becomes meeting arbitrary deadlines of procedures such as assessment, or correcting failures to supply the right answers to auditing questions. This is the substitution of failure demand for direct support or help. ('Failure demand' is a phrase coined by John Seddon in 1990. See below and the 'Afterword' and 'Books and Other Resources' at the end of the book.) Once you are caught up in the cycle of failure demand, reacting defensively with short-term, damage-limiting part-solutions for organisational compliance and survival, it is very difficult to break the cycle. You work from day to day and week to week trying to stem the tide of failure after failure, striving for the stamp of 'compliant' and appeasing everyone but your clients. Failure demand ties you to your office as you concentrate on conforming to outside requirements. It can happen that the person who has been neglected and on whom the current investigation and paperwork is concentrated has to suffer further neglect because the time for her care is being diverted into failure demand. How many times do you find yourself 'working at home' or in some way struggling to isolate yourself from the day-to-day life and work of your service in your attempt to get outside authorities off your back?

STANDARDS ARE BREACHED AT THE WILLOWS

When an inspection took place at The Willows, two new residents spoke to the inspector about television and food. The first observation was that there was a large TV in the front room but the residents weren't allowed to watch it. If a resident wanted to watch a favourite programme, they had to watch on a small telly in their own room. And the second gripe was to do with not being able to have what you liked for breakfast.

The inspector, quite properly, took both complaints seriously and approached a member of staff to explain. Karl, a fairly new member of the team, was asked and, at this early stage of his employment, was unable to give a satisfactory explanation. Yes, it was true that the main television was covered by a curtain when not in use, and weekday breakfasts were always the same: a choice of porridge, fruit, yoghurt, muesli, tea and coffee. But, being new, he didn't as yet fully understand the reasons why it was like this. Had the inspector asked a longer-standing resident or member of staff, he would have possibly got a fuller explanation, but the inspector felt that such important information should have been included in Karl's induction.

Later in the day, when giving feedback on the inspection to Gill, the inspector said that the residents were not able to make choices about their television viewing and what they had for breakfast, and the home was therefore non-compliant with the standards about choice, activities and food. He was also concerned that the induction programme for new staff didn't fully equip them for the job.

Gill gave the inspector a brief explanation that referred to decisions made by the whole community, and to her role as leader in sometimes guiding it to decisions that may at first appear to an outsider as counterintuitive. She also said that very occasionally she would make a decision that went against the community's choices, and then she had to face the whole group and argue her case. But, she said, the best way for the inspector to understand both these issues (the TV and breakfasts) would be to stay, join them for the evening meal and then give his feedback to the whole community. Everyone would know that an inspection had taken place so it would be the subject of discussion at the daily community meeting in any case. As to Karl's induction, Gill said that both staff and residents couldn't know everything in their first few weeks in the community. People learn as they live and work in the community; it takes time.

The inspector was unable to stay so late and, in any case, inspectors were discouraged from eating meals at places that they were inspecting. He liked The Willows and knew that it was a good home, so it was with regret that he felt he had to report the failure to comply with three standards.

While the core task of a care service can and should be simply and clearly stated, it would be wrong to assume that it is therefore a simple task. It is immensely complicated and subtle, and it isn't something that can be absorbed in a couple of weeks of induction. The better the service is, the more complex and variable it is. Social care is responding to people and situations through relationships. Inspectors, like many outsiders to social care, often find the practice of good care somewhat bewildering, and find it difficult to measure against standardised and general benchmarks. Furthermore, attempts to rate services in degrees of 'quality' will lead to more managers setting their own sights on gaining – or 'gaming' – good marks in inspection rather than on the core task.

As a manager, you should be leading a service that sets its own standards in how it provides good care. Your task is to lead good care for the people who need it. In doing so, your service is likely to be compliant with – and usually exceed – the standards set out by the regulator. However, you may bear in mind that regulators and the inspectors they employ do not always fully understand how social care works, or what the connections are between all the parts of a dynamic and changing psychosocial system.

Government, the regulator and the local authority, caught in the same cycle of 'failure demand', expect care services to demonstrate that they are marching to the beat of the current policy fad. For example, following some failure in care and pressure from the media and well-meaning charities, 'safeguarding' was highlighted as the missing element of care; so safety and safeguarding become what care services exist for. Such thinking leads to people being told to sit down because they may fall if they stand, and people being effectively locked in care homes because they may get run over in the street. And those crude but understandable reactions to highlighting safety as the priority in care work lead to a further round of safeguarding activities. Chief executives seem unaware of the absurdity of the oft-repeated mantra of care organisations: 'Our top priority is the safety of our users.' If safety really was the top priority, no one would go for a walk, boil a kettle, eat an ice-cream or a soft-boiled egg…and the bus in this book's preface could not move. A similar flurry of diversionary activity surrounds 'dignity': again a large amount of money is spent pursuing the chimera of dignity as if it were some unique and separate target that could be achieved through meetings, conferences, 'champions', 'agendas', and the production of endless turgid policies and 'putting procedures in place'. Soon to be followed by infection control, quality, excellence, 15-minute home care appointments, end-of-life care, compliance, nutrition, activities, and so on. These one-dimensional policy fads are driven by failure at some level, and government being subjected to media pressure (itself sometimes fed by specialist charities), leading to scapegoating lower down the pecking order. A central theme of this book is that good care is achieved by the leadership of the manager effecting whole-system change rather than by external initiatives and concentration on discrete aspects of the system which have attracted adverse publicity for government, providers or regulators.

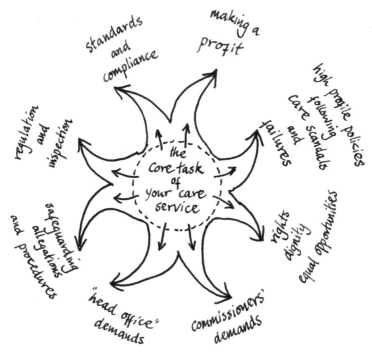

FIGURE 2.2 EXTERNAL DEMANDS DRAWING
THE CORE TASK OUT OF YOUR SERVICE

SHORT-LIVED PYROTECHNICS AS A DISTRACTION FROM THE CORE TASK

Government and its agents react to the exposure of failure by reaching for their box of policy fireworks. Each scandal has a rocket or Roman candle allocated to it. The BBC *Panorama* exposure of Winterbourne View in 2011 revealed to the general public what was going on in some private hospitals and care homes. It was a disgrace to the company, the management and the staff (obviously) but also to the regulator, which had failed to inspect the establishment properly and had ignored the whistleblower, to health and social care professionals outside the place who had neglected to check what was happening to people they sent and kept there, and to all the organisations that had a duty to check on what was going on. Consequently, the government and all other authorities and agencies involved indulged in a collective wringing of hands and laying of blame, countless meetings, reports and committees, hundreds of extra inspections, policies being fired off to demonstrate resolve, and three years later nothing had changed. Indeed, even more people were being exiled from their own areas to places like Winterbourne View than in 2011. The display had been spectacular but the next morning all that remained were sticks of rockets and the burnt-out shells of fireworks. The mountain roared and gave birth to a mouse.

The briefest of glances at the most recent history of poor and abusive care for people with learning disabilities shows government letting off one sparkling policy rocket after another – they climb high in the sky, explode…and disappear without trace. In 2006, there was a national scandal in Cornwall and the Health Secretary declared that she was taking steps 'to ensure it does not happen again'. To prevent something happening again, we need to understand why it happened in the first place, and to connect the event with its roots in the whole system.

THE 'FAILURE DEMAND' TRAP AND DIVERSION

When the core task is subverted or an externally defined task is substituted, the energy and focus of your service will dissipate into a downward defensive spiral. As manager, you will find that you spend your time reacting to failure: investigating and reporting on each example of failure. Safeguarding, disciplinary processes, medication errors, complaints, failures to respond positively the first time around: failure on failure on failure. In no time you will be managing only what has gone wrong and will continue to go wrong, because your service will now be in defensive retreat; its core task can never be achieved. There is insufficient time for good care because too much time is spent clearing up the mess from repeated failures, and you will never be able to lead.

INVESTIGATING AN ALLEGATION AT THE WILLOWS

Soon after Martha came to live at The Willows, her mother visited her at the weekend. Martha had enjoyed her first few days in the home, and was getting to know the staff and the residents.

Karl, who had now been at The Willows for six months, was working on the Saturday of the visit. He welcomed Martha's mother when she came to the door. When he introduced himself, she grasped his hand with both of hers and, gazing at him with evident admiration, she pulled his hand to her lips and kissed it. This left Karl feeling uncomfortable and wary.

Martha's mother also had learning disabilities and had lived in a children's home before being fostered when she was 11. At 15 she was pregnant with Martha. Well supported by her foster mother and social worker, she was a good mother to Martha as a baby and toddler, but had a series of partners, one of whom, it emerged later, sexually abused Martha. When Martha was a teenager and her mother was in her early 30s, they went out together like sisters and sometimes brought men home with them. They had enjoyed the company of some of these men but when Martha was 20, a man abused and exploited them, keeping them prisoner and prostituting them, and used their flat as a crack den. The flat was eventually raided by the police and social services were involved again.

Martha's mother had a stroke and lost the ability to walk. She went to live in a care home for older people, and Martha went to live at The Willows. After all they had been through, both mother and daughter continued to be naively trusting and positive. A fan of TV celebrity, reality and talent shows, Martha dreamed of romance, glamour and stardom. She did have a good singing voice and could also play the piano by ear, talents that she used to great effect later when she ran a singing group at The Limes while she was living in one of the flats at The Hub.

In the first couple of days at The Willows, Martha had looked at Karl in an adoring way and giggled a lot in his presence. It was unsettling and embarrassing for everyone, but Martha seemed oblivious to the disturbance she was causing. It was raised openly by residents with Martha in the daily meeting, and Karl talked with Gill and his colleagues about this. They had agreed that for now he should keep his distance as far as was possible in such a small community, and Martha's keyworker would spend as much time as possible with her. She would try to get Martha to join her and one of the other women to go horse riding at weekends.

Gill phoned Martha's social worker and, while alerting her to Martha's behaviour, she discovered more about her background than the social worker had hitherto disclosed. She also formed the opinion that the social worker was so outraged by the sexual exploitation and degradation of Martha (and her mother) that she had become a bit of a warrior on her behalf, and wasn't fully aware of how sexually provocative Martha could be. The sole focus for the social worker was Martha's safety and protection, and she was very fearful of her being harmed again by men. She had placed Martha at The Willows to be safe, but, as Gill explained to the social worker, while the residents' safety was important, it was not the core task of the community, and that had been made clear during Martha's assessment and placement. The social worker said she was surprised that any care home could fail to have safety as their top priority.

The discussion with Gill prompted the social worker to visit Martha's mother, who told her that she had been to The Willows, that Martha was very happy and getting along well. Asking her not to tell anyone, she confided that Martha had already got a very handsome boyfriend called Karl.

While the social worker knew that this allegation could be fantasy (on the part of Martha and her mother) she also felt that, given Martha's history and the potential for bad publicity following the media interest in the women's plight and the subsequent trial of the perpetrator, she had to make this a safeguarding issue. After consulting her manager, she contacted Gill and the Careshire adult safeguarding team. She told Gill that she expected Karl to be suspended while the allegation was investigated. Gill's response was that it was her decision whether to suspend Karl – and she would not – and that she had kept the social worker fully informed of Martha's behaviour. There was therefore no need to investigate this allegation. If Martha was to benefit from living at The Willows, this sort of diversion from the therapeutic plan – to enable Martha to grow and mature from living with and relating to others in the community – would undermine the core task. In addition, it would reduce the time and effort required from Gill to lead the community; it would remove Karl's work from the community and from the residents with whom he had special relationships, and would prevent Martha from facing and working through her relationship issues and feelings in and with the community. Gill still had to report the allegation to her manager, to the safeguarding team and to the regulator.

The result was that Gill had to spend the equivalent of several days' work investigating, reporting and justifying her decision not to suspend Karl to her manager, the safeguarding team and to the regulator. This was a severe setback to the work that The Willows needed to do with Martha and to the work of the whole community.

(This story continues in Chapter 4, 'Gill asks a client to leave The Willows'.)

Failure demand dominates many local authority adult care 'services', although there are few services as such. One way in which a department's performance is measured is by how many complaints are received and how quickly they are acknowledged and then responded to. There are assessors, referrers, commissioners and 'safeguarders' but local authority adult care services do not generally provide care. Their task has been transformed into handling complaints, rationing care and buying services – at the lowest possible price – for people whose needs are critical and, if not supported, will pose a serious risk to the local authority. So, people who need help are risk assessed on the basis of what might happen if their request for help was turned down and blame for a subsequent crisis or death were to be laid at the door of the local authority. In essence, it has become a reactive service instead of a responsive one. Many adult services are now motivated by the fear and discovery of failure rather than by the imperative of the positive core task of providing care and support to those in need. In addition, local authorities are charged with safeguarding, which is often manifested in the critical examination of failures in care that they have commissioned at the lowest possible price.

Another function of the commissioning side of local authority adult services is to 'quality monitor' the services it buys, so again, demand for your and your service's time and attention is triggered by a cycle of failure.

The constant churn of new defensive legislation, standards and guidance has forced managers to turn their attention to compliance with external requirements and away from the core task. It is because managers find it difficult to attend to the core task that failure at that level occurs. This is followed by further external demands resulting in even less attention to the core task.

DEMAND FOR EXCESSIVE RECORD KEEPING AT THE LIMES

The contract monitoring team from Careshire visited The Limes to review care plans. They sampled 20 plans and discovered that the records of 'hydration, nutrition and weight' were inconsistent between residents. Half the plans examined had no record at all, three had all three measures recorded, and the remaining seven had either one or two of the measures recorded.

They pointed this out to Gita who told them that records were kept only when there were concerns about drinks, food and weight and then a plan was made to attend to them. So, from the sample, for half the residents there was no current concern, for three there was concern in all areas, and for the others one or two of the areas of risk were being monitored. Of course they encouraged residents to eat and drink healthily, and in warm weather they were especially vigilant. What was normal for residents varied so much; some had been very slim all their lives and some were comfortably rotund.

But the monitoring team insisted that their standards required all residents to have their intake of food and drink recorded each day and to be weighed every two months. Gita always tried to avoid a direct confrontation on such matters, and assured them that the records were made – as they could see – whenever there was concern about hydration, nutrition and weight, and left it to them to decide what action to take about this apparent failure to comply with their required standards. She could see that they found themselves in a difficult position because they were bound by rules that did not fit the situation that was in front of them, and had been made to protect the local authority and not the client. She didn't rub salt into their bureaucratic wounds by adding that meeting their requirements might mean that the time spent with unnecessary recording would be better spent sitting, eating, drinking and talking with residents, in other words, better spent on the core task of care, and in this instance achieving good nutrition through relationships. Gita was also upset, but said nothing, by the monitoring methods used. Wouldn't it be better to come and have a meal (they would always be welcome), see what was going on, and then look at the care plans of anyone they were concerned about? That's how she would do it...come to think of it, that's how Gita and her team did do it: you respond to real need rather than work from a tick list of hundreds of possible needs. However, the monitoring team members were forbidden from eating meals in the establishments they were inspecting in case it could be construed as a bribe.

FINANCE, ADMINISTRATION AND 'HUMAN RESOURCES'

When we observe the workings of many care organisations, both within a service centre – for instance a care home – and in the head office, it is revealing to see how 'office' functions so often take precedence over the core task, when they should be supporting the core task. (See 'Turn it the right way up and it will work' in Chapter 6.) There is something about sitting in an office, in front of a computer, dealing with money, forms and administration that elevates its status above care work and leading care work. (What that 'something' is will be discussed in Chapter 3.) The job of administrator in a care home is sometimes seen as more important than that of a senior care worker or team leader. Similarly, there is a feeling, even amongst care staff and managers themselves, that head office staff, whether in finance, administration or human resources, are in a position to issue orders and demands. Of course these office jobs are important, but their importance should be measured by the contribution they make to supporting the core task, which is care, and those who carry out and lead the core task are the core personnel in any care setting. (See 'Connecting head office with the core task (Gita and the Limes)' in Chapter 7.)

Because 'office work' has this unwarranted higher status than care work or even than leading care work, managers are drawn into prioritising and separating office work. They begin to work 'office hours' and they spend the bulk of their time in the office. Yet, most social care managers' experience and training are in care and not in office work, and it is painfully obvious that they are no good at office work. Some heads of care homes sit for hours at computers they can't use properly; some can't even type, so a simple letter may take them an hour to compose. In larger social care settings, it makes sense to employ a competent administrator who can deal with all the routine clerical, administrative, financial and staffing jobs, and type a letter for the manager in double quick time. This is essential work and it can be very satisfying when the administrator is truly a member of the team, and clients and staff experience them as supportive and enabling rather than officious and superior.

HOUSEKEEPING, CATERING, MAINTENANCE

As with the administration of your service, if the vital work of providing good food and keeping the service clean and in good working order is either split off from or prioritised over the care work, the core task will suffer. Care takes place through relationships but frequently the most caring relationships are formed through the provision of some practical help or support. Food is an obvious example from infancy; the loving relationship between mother and baby is formed through the most basic essential care of food and physical comfort. In care homes, residents often form close relationships with housekeeping, catering and maintenance staff (see 'Mrs Smith's boundary issues at The Limes' in Chapter 4). Helping or providing in a practical way opens the door to friendship and emotional support, which is why we need to understand that a home care client will usually find it easier to accept practical help even when their most urgent need is emotional support. A care worker who arrives saying that she's come to listen to someone's problems is unlikely to do as well as if her reason for visiting is to prepare a meal, do the washing or help with getting up, and then the talking just happens.

In a care home or home care setting, it is always a mistake to split the care from the 'ancillary' jobs, and an even bigger mistake – as often happens – to contract them out. Housekeeping, catering and maintenance are part of care.

THE CORE TASK IS THE WHOLE TASK

After her first two years as General Manager at The Limes, Gita had earned an excellent reputation, not only with the residents and relatives but also with social care professionals and in the locality. Her local reputation and her professional competence were greatly enhanced by her membership of the Careshire Social Care Managers' Network (see Chapters 6 and 7). One of the many aspects of life at The Limes to have improved was the food and mealtimes. The chefs and the catering team had become integral to the home and took their full part in meetings and in making food central to care.

The Limes is run by a large care company with a good reputation. They now regard Gita as one of their 'star' managers and The Limes as a 'flagship' home, but the board of directors and even the managing director who had recruited Gita still didn't fully understand why The Limes was so good. When Gita had been with the company for two years, they appointed a new finance director who previously did the same job at a not-for-profit national provider. He came with a record of 'turning around' the finances of that organisation and one of his strategies was to 'outsource' the catering of the 26 homes to a well-known catering company. The caterers took over the kitchens and their teams, updated equipment, and introduced a common menu, suppliers, processes, and mealtimes across all the homes. According to the new finance director, this improved meals, complied with all the requirements of the regulator, and won praise from residents, staff and managers.

The food at The Limes was already excellent and Gita had even made savings on catering, which she had spent on setting up a workshop in the garden. When she started at the home all the catering and ordering had been centralised, and she'd had to persuade the company to let her take control of it because food and mealtimes were so important to how the home would develop.

The new finance director was appointed by the board with a promise that he could make substantial savings and improve the service by doing the same deal with a specialist catering company, only this would be even better value because there were more homes and the existing costs of catering were even higher than they had been at his previous organisation. He had also proposed that he would investigate outsourcing the housekeeping services for the homes, and suggested that quite spectacular savings could be made. When presenting the proposal to Gita and her colleagues at a company meeting, he said managers were particularly pleased to have the responsibility, risks and anxiety associated with catering taken away from them, and that one of the great advantages for them was that if catering was standardised in this way, the regulator would not be able to find one home compliant and another not. Indeed, the managers were able to tell the inspector during 'dignity and nutrition' inspections the exact nutritional value of every meal served.

Gita was outraged and said so. She felt betrayed by her regional manager and by her ally, Sarah, the managing director. She had spent time, thought and effort helping them to understand why food was such an important component of care (the core task) and why the manager must have control of the catering budget, kitchen and staff. She had written a short article for the company's newsletter that had subsequently been published in one of the social care trade magazines. And she had proved it to them by improving the food, integrating it with the whole life and care of the home, and by reducing waste and costs. The home was supplied by local firms with fresh meat, fish and vegetables, and these same suppliers contributed in other ways to the life of the home. The home was an important customer to them and they would often do special deals on seasonal foods. The chef planned menus from week to week in consultation with the residents, and with the local suppliers who kept him informed of stocks of special interest and value that would be available in the next week. These shops were also well known to many of the residents. At The Limes, helping in the kitchens on the group living units was an ordinary part of everyday life for some residents, as was picking fruit and vegetables from the garden, and collecting eggs from the home's chickens. So, while the main meals were cooked in the main kitchen, each of the units had basic ingredients to hand and were able to go out shopping for themselves. This sort of flexibility could not be built into a contract with an outside catering company.

Gita said the plan was not acceptable to her, and two colleagues at the meeting backed her up. However, most of the managers were prepared to accept this proposal, and felt that the advantages outweighed the disadvantages.

THE EXTERNAL PRESSURES AND DEMANDS FROM PROFESSIONAL BODIES AND 'IMPROVEMENT AGENCIES'

Good care cannot be achieved without staff support, training and development. However, the most significant professional development comes from the combination of direct experience with forms of supervision (see 'Supervision' in Chapter 3). For example, the stories and discussion in this book are of little use unless you, the reader, have your own experience to work with. For the stories to ring true and to be useful, you have to be able to say, 'Yes, that makes sense', or 'That was like something that happened to me', and the discussion must draw out and analyse the experience with the help of ideas, models and theories. A book or teacher that simply tells you what to think and how to do your job will be of little practical use or interest.

Of course, external resources (such as books, videos and training courses) can be immensely supportive and can – and do – contribute to your core task. However, their usefulness is dependent on who is serving whom. If you and your team are actively seeking out helpful training and development resources – if you are the customer in this relationship – you can select and make good use of the many excellent resources on offer to support the core task. But if you are constantly bombarded with the products of training organisations, some of which are telling you what you should and must do, what you must do for staff, what the contents of induction must be, and perpetually rejigging this and that qualification, neither you, nor your staff, nor your clients will benefit from the expensive agencies and quangos that produce this stuff. The situation is made worse by the alliance of these external organisations and their tendency to recruit staff from each other. They form a sort of aristocracy of social care – rich, powerful and incestuous, but lacking practicality.

Government rightly supports social care training with public money, but instead of being channelled through the people who would be able to pay the piper and be discerning when calling the tune, the money is channelled through the providers of training, so the only way to access it is to take what is on offer. (There is a parallel here with care providers and clients, and the advantages of direct payments so that clients can choose their own services.) Of course, the improvement agencies will argue that they are to a large extent employer-led bodies and therefore their output is in tune with what employers (social care providers) want. But here again we face the same problem of the employers, the improvement agencies, the regulators, the commissioners and the government telling managers what they need and how they should be inducting, training and developing their staff. Once set up, all these agencies have a vested interest in the perpetual production, reproduction and multiplication of new things for you to do and, to an extent, they have the power to make you do them.

Hanging on the coat tails of the improvement and auditing agencies are the training and consultancy companies and the colleges and universities who depend on the flow of new qualifications and new regulations for the continued existence of their social care departments.

GLORIA AND 4CS: SETTING UP AN APPRENTICESHIP AND TRAINING SCHEME WITH A LOCAL COLLEGE

Careborough Regional College runs a social care apprenticeship scheme. It is a major part of the college's activity and income. There are nearly a thousand apprentices in all their different schemes but only half of them complete the training successfully. For some social care providers, apprentices can be seen as a ready source of low-cost staffing and training with the possibility that once qualified, apprentices can join the team as permanent members of staff. Other providers use the scheme more creatively and make no distinction between pay rates for apprentices and permanent members of staff. Successful apprenticeship schemes depend on the quality of the working partnership between the employer and training provider.

4Cs experimented with apprenticeships for four care workers: two previously unemployed 18-year-olds and two older, experienced members of staff. They all completed their apprenticeships and qualifications successfully within 18 months, but the quality of the training and support from the college was poor. The tutors were not sufficiently experienced in social care and appeared to be too heavily reliant on text books and online resources. They were not reliable in attending meetings and assessments, and Gloria felt that she and her colleagues had to do most of the teaching. Gloria had spent many hours at the college attempting to improve the scheme, so she was surprised when the head of social care at the college proposed to her that 4Cs should take on 20 apprentices the next year. And the proposal was made in a way that implied that Gloria's criticisms and attempts to improve the training had had no impact whatsoever.

One of the problems was that some other employers seemed to be perfectly happy with the 'free' training that the college was providing and, along with paying their apprentices a very low wage, the scheme went a long way to 'evidencing' the staff training and development requirements of commissioners and regulators. It seemed that nearly everyone was happy with the scheme except Gloria.

Reluctantly, Gloria concluded that time and effort expended on working with the college in a way that would make the apprenticeship scheme worthwhile would undermine 4Cs' core task, so she turned down the proposal. However, Gloria was not rejecting apprenticeships themselves and saw them as having great potential, and fully recognised that training and staff development, including apprenticeships, were central to 4Cs' core task. She saw no future in working with Careborough Regional College at this stage. She resolved to bring the issue to the next meeting of the managers' network (see 'The Careshire Social Managers' Network' in Chapter 7).

DEFINING AND HOLDING ONTO THE CORE TASK

Social care services are set up to meet social care needs. A need – or usually a set of needs – demands a response (a person needs help) and the service is established in response. So the definition and development of the core task is emergent in response to the help and support which is asked for. With voluntary organisations, this may have started as an informal response to one, two or a few people and then grown. Small private providers often began with an owner/manager, family involvement and a small team of trusted staff. As they grow, organisations become more complex and parts of the task are split off into specialisms and, with the passing of time, the external legal, regulatory and bureaucratic demands multiply. The small, local, voluntary organisation may eventually grow into a national – even multinational – not-for-profit company. The owner/manager care business may be transformed over time into a big corporation with shareholders, a chief executive and a board of directors. Yet, in spite of this transformation, the managers of each service, the leaders of care on the ground, must hold on to and be guided by the core task. There will always be occasions when managers will be under pressure to allow the core task to slide off course, and will need to insist on getting it back on course.

A TROJAN HORSE AT THE HUB?

The Hub's task is to facilitate and host community groups and activities, including direct care. It is a multi-purpose community resource centre.

For some time, a large out-of-town supermarket has been contributing in several different ways to The Hub and its many activities and services. They send surplus food to the food bank; they supply prizes and shopping vouchers for the various clubs and social occasions; they have a staff volunteer scheme through which staff are encouraged and rewarded to give time. There's a corner in the superstore with a big banner proclaiming that the company 'Supports The Hub' with information leaflets about The Hub and all its activities and services. The leaflets have been printed at the supermarket's expense and bear its 'cheaper, better, fresher and trust us, we're your friend' strapline.

Over the years, as the supermarket has increased its support, Geoff has wondered if it could become counterproductive as everyone grows dependent on their help. 'We did it ourselves, and we do it for each other' is the spirit in which The Hub operates and the ethos at the heart of Geoff's leadership of the centre. He can't help feeling that the very local and strong community 'ownership' of The Hub could get lost amidst a back-door branding and a gradual insidious takeover by a multinational chain.

The Hub building and land are leased by a housing association from the council. The housing association converted the building from its original purpose (a care home) and built extra-care flats (on the upper floors) and a wide range of facilities on the ground floor. There's a large garden and car park, and a small sports area. It is quite a spread of valuable 'real estate'.

The chair of the housing association was for a short and traumatic time the chair of The Hub's management committee. She had attempted to change the whole ethos of the organisation, to make it more commercially orientated, resulting in the collapse of several groups and the eventual 'revolt' of the smaller community organisations which were based there. The chair resigned amidst much bad publicity, the former chair was re-elected and The Hub regained its communal strength, but Geoff suspected that the housing association chair was still scheming in the background to bring about the changes she failed to achieve as chair of The Hub (see 'Containing panic at The Hub' in Chapter 3).

While each organisation that uses The Hub has a distinctive core task, the overall purpose of the resource centre is a broad spectrum of community activities, events and social care. Some activities begin at the community and social end of the spectrum and some are very specifically focused on care. For example, the Thursday afternoon tea dance is social and is attended mostly by local pensioners, but half a dozen of the enthusiastic dancers keep their feet and toenails in good shape by attending the monthly foot care clinic, and four of the tea dancers go to the weekly 'memory club' for people with dementia. Both the foot care clinic and the memory club are run by trained volunteers. There are a number of local pensioners who attend once or twice a week to be helped with having a bath or shower, and then go on to join in various social activities.

So, when Geoff gets wind of informal discussions and a 'site visit' taking place between a local councillor, the council's head of finance, the finance director of the housing association and a couple of high-ups from the supermarket chain, his suspicions are roused.

Geoff asks himself a series of questions:

- What is the core task of The Hub?

- What is my role in leading that core task?

- What am I responsible for and to whom am I accountable for carrying out that responsibility?

- And, depending on my answers to the above questions, what should I do now?

Geoff refreshes his memory of The Hub's constitution and his own job description, and the answers lead him to alert key members of the management committee, including the chair, to the possibility that The Hub could be relocated and its core task could be undermined, diverted or diluted by talks that may be taking place at a higher level and behind closed doors. Previously, individual councillors were willing to conduct secret negotiations when they were closing the care home and hoping to sell off the building and land that The Hub now occupies, and there were rumours even then that this supermarket chain was interested in developing the site. It was only after a long campaign by local people that the council was shamed into acceding to the needs and ambitions of the community (see Chapter 6).

FORMATIVE CLIENTS: THE CLIENTS THAT HELP TO SHAPE AND CLARIFY THE CORE TASK

The influence of the clients on the core task is not often acknowledged. The task of a service as well as the practice is a joint project between the organisation and the people it serves. Since good care is a response to people's needs and situations and there is no 'standard' client, it follows that care is very strongly influenced by those who use it. Practice is emergent and becomes expert as clients' needs are responded to.

An organisation that starts by providing home care develops its expertise in relation to each client. The core task and its practice emerge and are refined and developed with each engagement. This is yet another reason for not imposing standardised practices and procedures from outside; they are best developed through experience.

The successful care of people with particular needs, personalities and histories shapes and clarifies the core task of a service. Too tight and precise a definition of your core task risks the danger of, on one hand, excluding people who would gain and contribute to the service and, on the other hand, including others who then find themselves being categorised in a way that restricts their potential. For example, some care homes that claim to specialise in dementia can turn out to be very dull and standardised institutions where residents are restricted by the label of dementia. People with dementia are as varied as the rest of the population, and dementia itself is a very broad category. It's a bit like segregating everyone under five foot six from everyone over that height, or everyone under 65 from everyone over.

Contrast such a specialist dementia care home with a small 'residential' home where someone with quite advanced dementia is living a good life, looked after by staff and other residents who are learning all the time about dementia from her. After giving very good care to this resident for a couple of years, and to several other people with dementia, the staff are far in advance of their equivalents at the specialist care home. The 'general' small home, which has learned from every resident is a much better place for someone with dementia than the big 'specialist' dementia care home that claims to know it all but imposes its 'care' regime and learns nothing from its clients.

SUGGESTIONS OF WAYS TO USE THIS CHAPTER

Here are some questions for discussion and activities to consider and discuss:

- Can you describe the core task of your service?

- How can you use your core task to improve your service?

- How can you use the concept of a core task with your staff, clients and other providers?

- Is the way you describe your core task different from the way your company/proprietor/employer would describe it?

- What are the threats to your core task? Internal? And external?

- Is it in danger of being corrupted and, if so, how?

- Consider Figure 2.2 and draw a sketch that applies exactly to your own service.

- Think about the impact, contribution and challenges that particular clients have made on your service and, in doing so, how they have shaped it to what it is now and may be in the future.

- Use the stories to compare with your own experience, and think about what you would do in similar circumstances:

  ○ 'Restoring the core task at The Limes'

  ○ 'Standards are breached at The Willows'

  ○ 'Investigating an allegation at The Willows'

  ○ 'Demand for excessive record keeping at The Limes'

  ○ 'The core task is the whole task'

  ○ 'Gloria and 4Cs: Setting up an apprenticeship and training scheme with a local college'

  ○ 'A Trojan horse at The Hub?'

3

BENEATH THE SURFACE
THE PERMANENT UNDERSIDE OF CARE

Good social care is given through relationships. It is 'feelings work' that takes place between individuals and groups within the context of an organisation. A good care service must be designed, managed and led in a way that not only takes full account of feelings, both conscious and unconscious, but works with and through feelings.

The concept and theory on which this book is based are that the social care service that you manage is a 'psychosocial system' operating on two levels. The 'psycho' level of the system underlies the rest of the system and most of it is 'beneath the surface'. The psychological level of feelings, beliefs and values, anxieties and defences, imagination and hope, is always there – but largely hidden – as the powerful driver of the 'social' level of the organisation's structure, rules and procedures, policies and planning, guidance and legislation.

The surface or social level of the organisation is deliberate but is not necessarily aware of what it is responding and reacting to, or defending against at the 'psycho' level beneath the surface. However, a good social care organisation is designed and managed to take full account of and to work with the feelings and psychological forces that are always present beneath the surface.

To identify two levels in this way is not to separate them. They cannot be separated because they are interdependent parts of a whole. To care is to feel. The organisation is steeped in feelings, and everyone's feelings (individually and collectively) are suffused with their experience of organisation (in its widest sense).

INDIVIDUAL FEELINGS

To try to understand what is going on at a deep psychological level with other people – the people you manage – you start with yourself. Although most of us recognise that our feelings play a very significant part in our lives – throughout our lives – for much of the time we are not fully aware of just what an influence these feelings have, of where they come from, or even what they are. Similarly our memories and thoughts hover in and out of consciousness and are feeding our imagination and sparking perpetual creativity. The involuntary workings of our minds can be exhilarating and productive, and can be deeply disturbing and depressing. We live our whole lives absorbing information and experience: remembering, imagining, communicating, feeling, creating, relating. We can't help but live in our minds as well as in our bodies. Our minds and bodies are not separate entities. We know that we have feelings in the tips of our fingers as well as in our hearts and heads. We find endless ways of avoiding, suppressing, diverting or calming our ceaseless imagination – TV, music, reading, sport, drink and drugs – but find that these, in themselves, also stimulate and engage our imagination.

When we sleep, we dream. Our minds go their own ways without our conscious control. Sometimes we wake, retaining just a fraction of some extraordinary scenario and we wonder where it came from…what does it mean? At other times we daydream; our minds take us somewhere, to a memory, a place, an idea, a hope, a feeling. There are deeply rooted – or, sometimes, deeply buried – feelings and experiences that make some people attractive to us and others repulsive, that draw us to a particular job, and that seem to dictate the decisions we make. 'Gut feelings' are those we don't quite know how to explain. Reason tells us one thing and our heart or gut tells us another. We speak of our minds 'playing tricks' on us. There is a constant interplay for all of us between what is rational and understandable and what is emotional and largely hidden, between the conscious and the unconscious, between what is on the surface and what lies beneath it.

If we accept that our emotions and unconscious minds are powerful forces in our lives, we must take them fully into account even if we can't control them. What is beneath the surface influences all our lives, our relationships and our work. Our imagination and creativity are what we work with.

We also live with conflicted and seemingly irreconcilable feelings. From birth to death we love *and* hate; we are sad *and* happy; we create and we destroy; we fight and we run away. The terms would have no meaning without their antonyms, and the feelings could have no existence without the presence of their opposites.

It would be impossible to provide good care for someone with dementia if you did not understand that memory, feelings and the unconscious played such significant parts in all our lives, and that dementia is likely to bring them to the surface in ways that can be disturbing, awkward and embarrassing, and revealing, perceptive, imaginative and witty as well.

WHAT YOUR CLIENTS BRING WITH THEM
AND
THE FEELINGS THAT YOUR SERVICE EITHER CONTAINS
AND MANAGES AND/OR DEFENDS ITSELF AGAINST
Loss anxiety fear isolation
Loss of physical and mental health
Loss of home spouse partner family place
Loss of position authority respect mobility
of energy taste sight hearing memory sense reason
intimacy relationship friendship
UNCONTAINED FEELINGS OF
VULNERABILITY PANIC DESPAIR DEPRESSION
DEPENDENCY DEATH
Love desire disgust hatred resentment regret shame
envy gratitude

FIGURE 3.1 THE FEELINGS BENEATH THE SURFACE

WORKING WITH NEEDS AND FEELINGS

Your clients, users, residents bring their needs and emotions with them. They also bring their imagination and creativity. They need all sorts of help and support (social care) and your service exists to meet these needs. Therefore any social care service engages with people's troubles, difficulties, losses, anxieties and disabilities. You must design, adapt and lead your service with this in your creative mind because without these needs there is no need for social care. A service that denies or rejects needs and the strong feelings that come with them is of no use; you work with need and feeling. Consequently, the work is always complex, difficult and demanding, and if you, as leader, are either not aware of or choose to ignore the power of the resulting anxiety to trigger unconscious institutional defences, your team and your care service will be unable to give good care.

LOSS

The need for social care usually arises from loss or absence. Your service exists to enable people to live their lives (and to die) in a way that is better for them. People need care because of a loss or absence of physical or mental health; of family, spouse, partner or carer; of social, emotional or practical support; of home. People's losses combine and multiply one on another, one leading to another in a downward spiral of loss. To give a simple example: someone loses their long-term partner; they become depressed; they stop eating properly; they stay indoors and lose their social contacts; they get ill, and so on. Bereavement is a universal and inevitable experience that always leads to some sort of emotional and practical readjustment for those who are bereaved.

The understanding that loss is change is based on a systemic interpretation. Our lives are not lived in separate compartments. Our beginnings affect our ends – our childhood, our adulthood, our old age, our family, our friends, our siblings, our relationships, our work, our home. Each loss is both a gap and an opening. We mourn and we, sometimes, move on…and sometimes we don't. Loss of a partner may open up a new life, and it may close down an old life. Loss of mobility, through a fall for example, would seem unlikely to lead to new adventures, but it can lead to discovering and developing different sorts of mobility and new interests. And loss of mobility can also be utterly devastating physically and emotionally. The onset of dementia is as yet irreversible and is often described by family and carers as the 'loss' of the real person, yet there are couples and families who do genuinely 'live well' with dementia and, difficult as it is, adapt their lives and relationships to accommodate the losses.

UNCONTAINED FEELINGS AND THE NEED FOR CONTAINMENT

Some of the extreme emotions people experience are terror, rage and despair, leading to panic. Imagine a baby in a fit of apparently uncontrollable yelling and crying, and imagine holding that baby so these overwhelming feelings can be contained – accepted, held, comforted and loved. Someone (often the mother) takes control *for* the baby. Imagine also – or recall for yourself – how frightening one's own feelings of resentment and even hatred, and of incompetence, impotence and panic can be when trying to calm (contain) a crying infant, especially when one is physically and emotionally exhausted. Unless you can to some extent contain or calm your own emotions, you are unlikely to be able to contain (calm) a baby's rage and despair. Reason seems to vanish; it is all raw emotion and trying to find that capacity in oneself to love, cherish and comfort a howling, kicking bundle of rage and pain.

Yet if you are able to observe the situation even while you are immersed in it and thereby to understand this system (you and the baby), you do find the capacity to contain. That ability to observe and understand yourself – your own emotional responses – and your context comes from your own experience of containment – of being held – as a baby, an adolescent and as a grown-up. The process of containment between mother and child enables the child to grow emotionally, mature, think and experience itself as a whole, separate person. If, as a carer – or care worker – one feels held, supported, understood – contained – one can usually find the personal resources to provide the containing elements of care that are so vital to good care. And you, as a manager, and the care service you manage, will contain the feelings that may threaten to overwhelm both clients and workers, thereby enabling the organisation to learn and mature, and apply itself to the core task.

So we can think of the care service as a 'container' in physical and emotional terms. Containment in this sense does not mean restriction or incarceration. For example, a care home that is well built, feels welcoming, clean and comfortable, and is secure against intrusion will serve to contain residents' anxieties. Even more importantly, calm and friendly staff who know what they are doing, are not frightened of and do not avoid the residents' difficulties, pain and chronic needs, and who are evidently part of a team which is supported and led by you (the manager), will convey a powerful message of therapeutic containment. It is from this experience of settled security and confidence that one can begin to tolerate and accept one's frailty and vulnerability, and live *with* them rather than deny them.

If a home care client can rely on and trust both the person who gives the care and support, and the organisation that employs their carer, that client will experience a level of containment that makes their emotional and practical needs tolerable.

CONTAINING PANIC AT THE HUB

Before Geoff had been able to have a full discussion with the chair of the trustees at the Hub about the secret meetings taking place between the supermarket, the council and the housing association, word had got out.

On Friday evening, Geoff received phone calls, emails and texts from a wide variety of extremely anxious and angry group leaders, staff and Hub users. Some, who didn't know Geoff well, accused him of being complicit in the plan. (The rumour of secret meetings had already assumed the status of a determined plan to sell off The Hub to commercial interests, including the supermarket chain.) People were worried about the community groups and services that they had fought so hard to set up and maintain; those who were employed were worried about their jobs; and there was a general feeling of being oppressed, exploited and undervalued...again.

Edwin, who worked at The Hub and lived at The Willows, had gone home on the Friday evening after he heard the rumours and told everyone that The Hub was closing and he was losing his job. He didn't go to work the next Monday.

The Hub was open for several groups and events over the weekend, which provided the opportunity to spread the rumour more widely. Geoff, who made a practice of being there at some time most weekends, decided this was a weekend that he would have to go in. By this time he had spoken further to the chair. Geoff was upset to be accused of being part of the sell-out plot and wanted to clear his name. After all he'd done and been through to stay true to The Hub's core task, to be accused of this treachery was very hurtful and unjust. As he talked it over with the chair, he began to understand where these feelings, both his and those of the people accusing them, came from.

As a local community resource that was working well and involving hundreds of people, many of whom came there because they had never had or had lost other sources of support (work, income, family, partner, friends, health and mobility, etc.), The Hub was full of the dispossessed. A rumour (based on real events) that their source of support and cohesion was to be taken from them by people and organisations that represented those who had taken everything else from them but on whom they were still to some extent dependent, created rage and panic. In one way, the reaction was a measure of just how important The Hub was and how well Geoff was leading it. This was the gist of his conversation with the chair, who helped Geoff to contain his shock and anger at finding himself accused of conspiring to sell off The Hub. He could now help the others to contain their feelings and, using their feelings, work together to stop this plan before it ever got started.

So, Geoff went in on Saturday and stayed most of the day talking with anyone who wanted to talk. He and the chair planned an open meeting for Monday evening by which time he had phoned Edwin and a few others who had not been contacted over the weekend, and the panic was contained, the feelings expressed and shared and channelled into practical action.

THE FEAR AND DENIAL OF DEPENDENCY AND VULNERABILITY

The fear of dependency has its roots in infancy and stays with us all our lives. It is a permanent anxiety that underlies organisational, national and international relationships. The fear of dependency pervades society, culture, economics and politics. Having grown up and achieved a state of adult independence, we fear the time when we may yet again be dependent through physical or mental ill health, disability or frailty. Beneath the declared policies and professional objective of helping people to achieve independence lies the fear and denial of dependency and vulnerability. It is of course a fantasy to suppose that we are at any stage of our lives fully independent of other people; we all live through episodes of greater and lesser dependency.

Becoming aged and frail is frightening enough without adding the possibility of dementia, incontinence and immobility. Seen from a social/psychological perspective, 'ageism' (prejudice against older people), like other prejudices, is generated by fear and denial. What we fail to acknowledge and fear in and for ourselves, we identify and fear in others. Older people – and especially dependent older people – remind us of our own impending decline and mortality. As we get older we fight against the inevitable, and when we are younger we tend to avoid contact with vulnerability. Such basic psychological defences are reinforced and institutionalised in our culture and economy. So older people are demeaned as unproductive in a world that values production and economic growth. Materially unproductive people are characterised as a burden on the economy, and dementia is portrayed as a 'time bomb' which will destroy our society. This dystopian scenario depicts a future with too few productive people to pay for the useless mass of sick and ageing pensioners, yet the same hostile projections serve to exclude immigrants of working age who could fill the supposed gap between productivity and dependency.

CONTAINING ANXIETIES IN SOCIAL CARE ORGANISATIONS

In the same way that an individual fights off or defends him- or herself against anxiety, so does an organisation. These are usually unconscious defences (beneath the surface), which manifest themselves (on the surface) both in consciously planned, formal procedures and in informal – sometimes illicit – arrangements between staff members. Just as an individual may treat a client in a cold and impersonal way because their loss or disability is somehow so painful or threatening that the care worker becomes aloof and uncommunicative, so may a whole staff team work with an ethos of detachment combined with group collusion to avoid talking about clients as real people like them, and to talk over them as if they didn't exist.

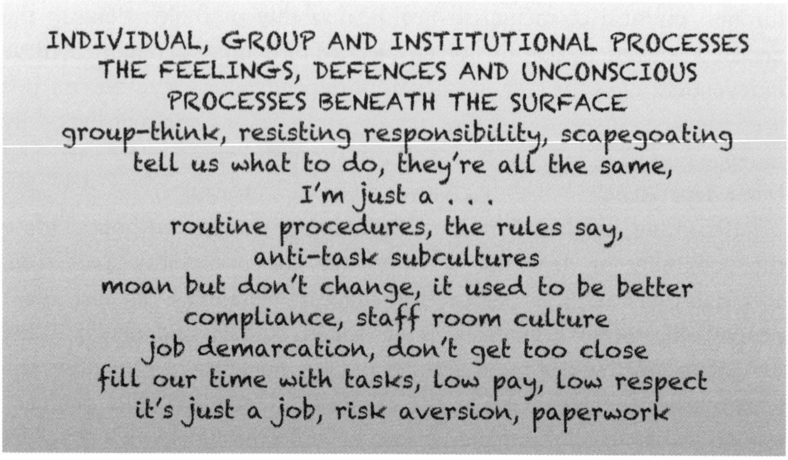

INDIVIDUAL, GROUP AND INSTITUTIONAL PROCESSES
THE FEELINGS, DEFENCES AND UNCONSCIOUS
PROCESSES BENEATH THE SURFACE
group-think, resisting responsibility, scapegoating
tell us what to do, they're all the same,
I'm just a . . .
routine procedures, the rules say,
anti-task subcultures
moan but don't change, it used to be better
compliance, staff room culture
job demarcation, don't get too close
fill our time with tasks, low pay, low respect
it's just a job, risk aversion, paperwork

FIGURE 3.2 FEELINGS, DEFENCES AND UNCONSCIOUS PROCESSES

SOME COMMON INDIVIDUAL, GROUP AND ORGANISATIONAL DEFENCES...

...to defend against the anxiety engendered by clients' needs and inherent in good care. The anxieties that provoke these defences are always present below the surface in social care. They come with the core task and, therefore, if you as manager do not create a containing supportive framework for staff, deliberate and unconscious anti-task defences and practices will undermine your service.

- **Group-think**: everyone thinking the same; suppressing difference, and blocking questioning; adopting one-dimensional, superficial explanations for poor care or low morale that absolve the group from accountability.

- **Resisting responsibility**: always opting for the easy answer rather than taking responsibility and *thinking*; knowing that something is wrong but not accepting that you have a part in putting it right – 'I can't use the hoist because the night staff didn't put it on charge.'

- **Scapegoating**: picking on an individual to blame for what's going wrong and persecuting them in order to avoid personal and group culpability – the 'slow' member of staff who won't hurry people, the worker who seems to have favourites and gives special attention to some and not to others, the colleague who is a bit different and doesn't go along with the group.

- **Tell us what to do**: refusing to think for oneself and take the initiative; demanding to be given orders – 'Nobody told me I had to sit down when I'm feeding someone.' 'This toilet is dirty. The manager should tell someone to clean it.'

- **They're all the same**: using 'they' to refer to your clients, depersonalising your clients and characterising them as all having the same needs – 'They can be very aggressive; never crouch down in front of them.' 'They don't like foreign food.' 'They don't know what's going on and they don't notice when someone dies.'

- **'I'm just a...'**: refusing to acknowledge the importance of your role and the responsibilities that go with it – 'I'm just a care assistant; I'm not paid to think.' 'I'm just a support worker; I do as I'm told and get the work done.' 'Don't ask me; I don't make the rules.'

- **Routine procedures**: doing everything by rote or 'by the book' – 'It's my break time; I'm entitled to a 20-minute break.' 'Time to do the toileting.' 'I'm on bathing this afternoon.' 'I'm doing the medication; count me out for the next two hours.' 'I arrived on time, gave the medication, signed the book and left. That's what it says in the care plan.' 'It's 6.30a.m.; haven't you finished the early teas yet?'

- **The rules say**: taking refuge in 'the rules' to avoid using your judgement, and some of the rules quoted do not exist – 'No, you're not allowed to talk about your family to clients.' 'You must wear gloves for all personal care.'

- **Anti-task subcultures**: exclusive groups and cliques forming to undermine the core task by using informal and illicit methods and ways of working – 'We're the A team; we get the work done and then we have fun.' 'Let's go and have a smoke.' 'You do my baths and I'll do your toileting.' 'Let's get the residents to bed early and then we can relax.'

- **Moan but don't change**: forever criticising and complaining about a service but never being willing to propose and enact change – 'We're always short-staffed and these new staff have taken my overtime.' 'The residents stay too long over lunch.' 'They (in the office) have no idea what we put up with but I don't want them coming snooping around our jobs.'

- **It used to be better**: always harking back to some supposedly better time and thereby undermining any positive efforts to make progress – 'Remember when we used to have a Christmas party for all the staff, and when X got drunk and had a fight with Y.' 'We used to be able to go off early on a Friday.' 'The residents liked it better in those days, when the old matron was here.'

- **Compliance**: uncritically accepting and conforming to external demands and instructions rather than using your own judgement and principles – 'The inspector told us that all care plans had to...' 'Quality Monitoring need this form filled in every week.' 'When in doubt, report it to safeguarding.' 'Head office say we've got to...'

- **Staff room culture**: staff getting together and sharing a negative culture – look at the noticeboard and the anonymous notes, cartoons, posters. What is the state of the staffroom? Dirty mugs and plates left around? What is the underlying message and effect of the room?

- **Job demarcation**: not doing something that needs doing because it's not in your job description – 'Not my job, mate.' 'I just do as I'm told – I'm not paid to think.' 'My union tells me I'm not insured to change light bulbs.'

- **Don't get too close**: keeping a distance between you and your clients in order to protect your feelings – 'Don't get over-involved.' 'Be professional.' 'Protect yourself.' 'Don't get too fond of people who are going to die soon.' 'Don't have favourites.'

- **Fill our time with tasks**: being perpetually busy (but often to not much effect) in order to avoid reflecting, feeling and thinking – 'Sorry, no time to talk.' 'We'll have to postpone supervision.' 'We're too busy to have a handover, but you all know what to do.' 'Got to get the baths done.' 'I've got ten care plans to update before I go off duty.'

- **Low pay, low respect**: resisting taking on responsibility and taking a pride in your job – 'We're the lowest of the low.' 'I'd earn more in Tesco.' 'I don't tell people where I work because they'll think I'm abusing the service users.' 'Pay peanuts, get monkeys.'

- **It's just a job**: keeping your feelings and commitment at bay, and pretending that you are only here for the pay.

- **Risk aversion and misusing risk assessments**: avoiding taking the risk of taking a risk while pretending that it is in your client's best interests, or the decision is out of your hands; using risk assessments as decision makers, rather than using them to assist with making a decision.

- **Paperwork or computer work**: taking refuge from the task by filling in forms or sitting at the computer, often 'busy' with paperwork that doesn't need doing; frequently those who escape into paperwork are not competent writers or computer users, and complain bitterly about having to do it.

IDENTIFYING AND DISMANTLING DEFENCES AT THE LIMES

When Gita first took over as manager of The Limes, she found the home was infested with institutional defences against anxiety. It was how the home functioned. It did not surprise Gita, nor did she attempt to dismantle these defences by simply taking them away because she knew that would be like hoeing off deeply rooted weeds: two more would spring up where one had been before. With staff, she would find and acknowledge the roots of the defences, deep beneath the surface of the home and its work.

Gita started by exposing herself to the same emotional and practical stresses that staff had adapted to and had found a way to tolerate under cover of these unconscious defences. She worked with them. She worked alongside all the staff, doing the same jobs during the same shifts, and this triggered resistance at all levels in the organisation, inside and outside The Limes.

Her regional manager and virtually all senior head office staff were angry with her. With a change of manager and two years since the previous inspection, an inspection was overdue. Their argument was that, with the regulator breathing down their necks, improving The Limes was urgent. There were all sorts of policies, procedures, records and care plans to be updated and put in place to prepare for an imminent inspection, and this wouldn't get done with Gita pretending to be a care assistant or cleaner or kitchen assistant. Anyway, she wasn't paid five times as much as them to work at their level. Her fellow managers were also outraged by Gita's approach; they felt it would undermine her authority and, by association, theirs.

The only ally that Gita had amongst the hierarchy and her peers was Sarah, the managing director who had appointed her, and even she felt pretty queasy about it as the pressure built on her to put a halt to Gita's seemingly subversive initiative.

Amongst the senior staff in the home there was further resistance. Why should they continue to do all the management tasks that Gita should have been relieving them of? She was paying more attention to the basic grade staff than to them, and they needed just as much help.

And the staff with whom Gita was working were initially deeply anxious about having her by their side while they cared, cleaned, washed and cooked. Suddenly they felt under intimate scrutiny. Gita was seeing things that were done but never got talked about. But, within days, they were talking about the work, their feelings, their frustrations and unhappiness, and sometimes about the hopes and ambitions they once had for giving good care. While making a bed or emerging from a room after washing a dying resident, a care worker would be in tears...and they talked, and Gita listened. For many, it was such a relief that Gita was there witnessing the work and the feelings that previously could not have been acknowledged, let alone expressed.

However, at the head office level, it was as if someone of the same status – a colleague – was doing their dirty washing. As if she could see, smell and touch their soiled underclothes and bed linen; she was privy to their grubby secrets. They paid other people to do that: people who depended on them for a job and who had no interest in their intimate personal lives. But with the aim of leading good care at The Limes, Gita was doing this to bring to the surface some underlying and shameful truths about the company and its homes. She was sorting through their bins and it was exposing, frightening and threatening. This is what the lower paid staff in the home were exposed to every working hour, what residents had to live with, but what head office staff convinced themselves did not exist.

The senior staff in the home were understandably resentful and envious of the attention that Gita was giving to the others. They too were unhappy and frustrated by the way The Limes worked. They had put up with and tolerated the previous manager's lazy and dictatorial reign. They were implicated. They had had to flatter and collude with her to survive, and now Gita had swanned in and was seeing the shameful results. They too would have liked to have been able to do what Gita was doing; she would get all the credit and they would get all the blame.

The Limes began to change at a deep level as soon as Gita did her first shift working alongside the care staff, and it went on changing at an increasing pace and at a deeper level every day of the three months that she spent on shifts, but this was just the first dramatic phase of change.

The inspector did return in Gita's first two months, and although it was a different inspector from the one who had found The Limes to be 'fully compliant' two years previously, the official verdict of this inspection had to be 'requires improvement'. The paperwork was still at best patchy and at worst non-existent. Only a few of the policies and procedures had been updated. Care plans were still in a state of being redesigned. Many care staff, residents and their relatives told the inspector how much better things were since Gita came, but a few told of breakdowns in routine and order. Some staff and residents who had been at the home for years had found ways of surviving there and even prospering, and were frightened by Gita's radical approach. Other than the testimony of staff, residents and relatives, the inspector could find little hard evidence of improvement. The home was 'non-compliant' on several standards and a requirement for an improvement action plan was demanded.

The inspector was sympathetic to the changes Gita was making but had to assess what was on the surface, and Gita was working with what was beneath the surface. The inspector was looking a couple of months ahead, and Gita was looking years ahead.

Gita knew that this sort of change is hard to sustain and that there are periods of setback before moving forward again. While the three months of Gita's initial participant research (working shifts) was hopeful and stimulating for staff, when she produced a review based on her experience, it signalled a period of depression in the home as staff (and residents to some extent) came to terms with how bad things had been. Now they had to make a choice between continuing with this physically and emotionally exhausting process of change and leaving things to settle back into old patterns of defensive, institutionalised behaviour, which, after all, was only there to protect staff and the home from the emotional challenge and battering that the work itself was causing, and appeared to be more acceptable to the regulator.

For a few staff, there was still hope and expectation, and they had the energy and commitment to see it through. For most there was weariness and fear of failure, feelings that were confirmed by the inspection report. It was then very difficult for Gita to maintain the initiative for fundamental change that she had started. Again, but now with the backing of an adverse inspection report, almost everyone in the organisation felt vindicated in their initial criticisms of Gita's strategy for change: her naive commitment to the core task, her foolish tactic of working beneath the surface and her arrogant assertion that she knew what she was doing. While Gita's predecessor was succeeding in papering over the cracks in her new home, using long-established management tactics, The Limes was apparently going from bad to worse.

Although, when accepting the job, Gita had told Sarah (the managing director) that real change would take at least two years before outsiders started to recognise a change for the better, Sarah needed quicker results to justify the change in direction in which she was trying to lead the company.

Fortunately for Gita, she had alternative sources of support: her own knowledge of institutional defences and, most importantly, she had made contact with her fellow managers, Gill and Geoff, and Gloria who was even then setting up the Careshire Social Care Managers' Network (see Chapters 6 and 7).

ANTI-TASK PROCESSES AND DEFENCES IN THE WIDER SYSTEM
'Putting procedures in place'

Clients and staff appreciate a well-ordered, reliable service providing the therapeutic framework within which good care relationships flourish. However, some orderly and efficient care services do not promote good care; they promote order, efficiency and compliance with external demands, and they impose a 'care regime' that is reactive rather than responsive. Instead of doing the right thing – the core task – they do the wrong thing righter: a more efficient 'delivery' of everything but the core task.

The difference between these two types of care service can be illustrated by approaches to (in)continence in a care home. 'Desperate' is a common word used to describe what it feels like to need to go to the toilet urgently. When you are immobile and away from your own home, this word should be taken literally: despairing and in great distress. In one home, there will be a rigid, two-hourly 'toileting procedure', which is designed to reduce smells, and uses incontinence pads and other equipment to prevent the wetting and soiling of clothing and furniture. The procedure copes with the results of incontinence (which is better than not coping with them) but does not help those who suffer from incontinence to become continent.

In another home, there is no 'toileting procedure', but each individual resident is helped to be continent by a totally individual approach. There is careful observation, there is empathy and there is systematic help with this most distressing and undignified condition. Following their approach to all problematic situations, first staff and resident seek to understand the problem. Typically, they find out what is happening, why and when. Usually, within days – sometimes hours – of investigating the problem, they begin to manage it. Anyone can become incontinent if, for whatever reason, they can't get to the toilet in time and, for nearly everyone, bladder and bowel control is a matter of diet, habit, time, mobility and health. Without needing to be told, staff adapt their work to the client's needs. The difference between the two approaches is the difference between an imposed system (putting procedures in place) and a systemic response to particular need. Good care is created by designing and building practice from the core task.

To 'put procedures in place' is a phrase that is commonly used as a response to some failure of care. It is based on the widespread misunderstanding that good care is achieved through the imposition of standardised procedures. Sound procedures are created from practice, not the other way round. Any procedure is only as good as its practice, and wherever procedure and practice differ, one or both need changing. Moreover, we should always question the use of a procedure and the motivation for 'putting it in place'. Does this procedure support good practice, or does it take discretion and judgement (responsibility) away from the client and care worker? Does it come between the client and the service, defending staff and the organisation from the anxiety associated with caring, and serving as a defence against external criticism? A common manifestation of the 'procedures in place' defence is a file or files of paperwork specifically prepared for external examination by inspectors, commissioners or 'quality assurance' assessors. Rather than trusting the practice and day-to-day reality of the service to speak for itself, it is presented in a dressed-up, edited form that is easy to digest and always – to some extent – wishful thinking, if not downright lying.

Standardised procedures are used as a protective barrier (defence) between the organisation and the anxieties provoked by its core task. To be 'compliant' your care service has to have a long list of standard and acceptable procedures in place. The external bodies such as the regulator or commissioner accept the evidence of the file of procedures as an assurance or promise that this is what the organisation does – what the real practice is – and, if it turns out to be false evidence, it is the provider organisation that is guilty of misrepresentation. The provider organisation can get every member of staff to countersign the procedure to verify that they have read and understood it, so that, if they fail to put the procedure into practice, it is a disciplinary issue, not the provider's fault. The member of staff can fall back on procedure to avoid the difficult decisions and dilemmas that are so often posed by the care relationship. And, even at the level of the client, procedures are misused to avoid confronting difficult personal issues between the client and the care worker. So the imposition and acceptance of standardised procedures for care has the effect of making it difficult for the care worker to respond authentically to the client's needs and wishes, of blaming care workers when they deviate from procedures and of denying accountability at a higher level in the organisation when care fails.

Castlebeck used a 'putting procedures in place' defence, commenting, 'We were shocked when *Panorama* contacted us with these allegations on 12 May 2011 and shocked that this alleged behaviour had not been detected via the whistle-blowing policy that the company had in place.' Castlebeck's response to the *Panorama* exposé of Winterbourne View, an establishment that was found to be fully compliant by the regulator and had all procedures in place including, ironically, a whistle-blowing policy which had itself been inspected and found to be compliant.

Denial

When the bad feelings associated with caring for sick, vulnerable, dependent and dying people are not acknowledged and worked with, they are denied. It is common to hear care workers profess their pure caring feelings, but very uncommon to hear them admit to having hateful and cruel feelings about those they care for. Indeed, in many care settings, it may lead to dismissal. So, what are they to do with those feelings?

The situation is made worse for them by the refusal to accept such feelings at any level in the organisation, and to read and hear that the company boasts of how perfectly caring they and the organisation are, when they know from their daily experience that they are not.

So the underside of care is denied at every level. At every level, the pretence of perfect care must be repeated. No one at the top of a company wants to hear the truth, from a care worker whistleblower, or from a manager who is leading change.

> Our Care team approaches and philosophy include providing: Reassuring and highly trained staff for support and assist [sic] in raising self-esteem. Assisting in activities of daily living – life skills. Assisting in making choices, maintaining dignity, upholding rights and privacy. Assisting and providing a fulfilling life where individuals have a safe, secure and homely environment where life is enjoyable and free from stress or anxiety.
>
> (Anglia Retirement Homes Ltd website, April 2014)

In April 2014 the BBC's *Panorama* exposed abuse at The Old Deanery, Anglia Retirement Homes, and this was their response:

> We are shocked and saddened by allegations made by the BBC's Panorama programme of inappropriate behaviour by some members of staff at The Old Deanery Care Home and apologise unreservedly for those failings. We care passionately about our residents and will not tolerate this kind of behaviour. These incidents involved a small number of staff and are not reflective of the high standards of care which we expect and demand from all of our team. As soon as the new management team was made aware of the allegations we took immediate action. We hired an independent law firm to carry out a full investigation as a matter of urgency. Eight staff were immediately suspended, and have not returned to work, pending a full inquiry.
>
> (Statement from Anglia Retirement Homes Ltd, 30 April 2014)

In a letter to *Caring Times* (June 2014), I wrote:

> Having watched yet another expose of care homes (*Panorama* 30th April) and heard the renewed determination of all and sundry to put a stop to neglect and abuse wherever it occurs, I am saddened and frustrated by the continued failure of government and the social care establishment to FEEL and THINK, and accept responsibility.
>
> The potential for neglect and abuse is inherent in care, whether at home in a family or in a care home. When it comes to the difficult job of caring – paid or unpaid – there are no pure, caring feelings. Everyone has good and bad feelings about caring. We are human and flawed. Most of us, most of the time, can manage to keep the bad feelings in check. But, put us to work in an understaffed care home on low wages, without training or respect, without good leadership, joining a gang of staff who have been institutionalised and working with a mass of residents who themselves have been deprived of love and respect, serving a company that aims to make a fat profit out of this situation, and those bad feelings will overwhelm all but saints.
>
> We will see regional managers, and inspectors, and local authority contract monitors telling the company that this home is 'compliant'; the dishonest claims to 'person-centred' care from the company; the local authority placing people in this awful institution and knowingly paying less than good care costs. And then we have to watch the minister, the regulator, the local authority, and the employer wringing their cleanly washed hands over the situation they have created, ignored and now blamed on us.
>
> The solution? First acknowledge that good care cannot be commanded, controlled and 'delivered'. Know that caring evokes bad feelings as well as good in us all. Therefore run homes in a way that helps staff to understand and manage those bad feelings and don't add further bad feelings by treating them like shit.
>
> Give good, principled leadership – registered managers who will fight all comers on behalf of residents and staff. Pay properly for the job you want done; support and train. Create care that is locally based and accountable. Stop telling people what to do and how to do it, when you (government downwards) don't know how to do it and seem to have forgotten what it feels like to care. That will be a good start.
>
> (John Burton, Independent Social Care Consultant)

Personalisation

Personalisation – so called – can be a procedure to be put in place or a risky but positive change of relationship, but there's no need to make what is already a fundamental value and part of good care into a separate process. Good care has to be personal, just as it has to be dignified, and many aspects of care have to be private.

As a government policy, personalisation was promoted to give all users of social care services an individual budget, and to give some people the money for their care and support in direct payments so that they could choose and buy their own services. This policy makes sense and has led to some changes, including the reduction in local authorities' use of 'block contracts' (or bulk buying), whereby they negotiated so many hours or 'beds' from providers in return for a reduced fee, which forced people to use substandard services and put many good, small providers out of business.

As a procedure, many far from personal activities take place in the name of personalisation. For example, 'personalising' the contents of a resident's bedroom in a care home. So one might find in an inspection report, 'Some residents' rooms had been personalised with family photographs and ornaments. This ensured that the individuality of residents was maintained.' One can imagine the personalisation procedure being put in place in the care plan: 'Room 33 personalisation rating?' Used like this, personalisation appears to have the opposite effect to the one intended, and becomes a defence against the threat of individual and non-conformist preferences.

Similarly, residents' 'person-centred' care plans are checked to see if they've participated in making the plan by signing it or if there is some record of how the plan was made with them. This is like a financial institution reading out some get-out clause or disclaimer before they sell you a 'bespoke product' that they claim will be just the thing to secure your finances for life.

Almost any aspect of good, individual care could be classed as person-centred. Used like this such words serve to distance and proceduralise, and thereby to defend against the anxieties engendered by the individual, close, personal attention and relationship that is at the heart of good care.

During a television exposé of a care provider in 2014 (quoted above), which claimed (along with many other providers) to be 'person-centred', a resident said, 'They treat me like shit, but I'm not shit, I'm a person.' So much for that sort of 'personalisation' and 'person-centred' care.

Personalisation can also mean what it was originally intended to mean: putting people in charge of their own care, thereby changing the relationship between clients and care providers. The problem with such 'agendas' (the 'personalisation agenda') is that they are proceduralised; the procedure is ticked when completed, and the good intention is lost amidst the institutionalised practice. Such practice is a defence against the anxiety engendered by putting clients in charge of their own care.

Risk aversion

Risk aversion is avoiding taking the personal risk of taking a risk while pretending that one is acting in the client's best interests rather than one's own. Risk assessments are sometimes used as procedures to make decisions – a version of 'the computer says No' – as if it's possible to feed the information into the form as an equation. The calculation will be made and there will be no need for a human being – usually the manager – to make a decision. In most social care services, there are scores – sometimes hundreds – of risk assessments for every piece of equipment, every substance and every action. In addition, there will be individual risk assessments for every aspect of each client's life. People are prevented from doing quite ordinary things, like pouring a cup of tea or buying a paper, because a risk assessment has not yet been completed. It is illogical and deeply institutionalising, yet it has become standard, required practice in social care aimed at protecting the provider organisation. Risk assessments are yet another record to inspect and thereby judge the compliance of care services. They are misused as yet another defence against the anxieties inherent in the core task.

A FAILURE TO ASSESS RISK AT THE WILLOWS

The residents at The Willows have a community meeting each day after the evening meal. It is an informal meeting and not everyone is there every day, but important issues and events are discussed and decisions are made. A community meetings book is kept on the sideboard to record each meeting: who's there, broadly what is discussed and any decisions made. Sometimes a resident writes the record and sometimes a worker because not all residents can read and write, but everyone is informed of what took place at the previous meeting.

For several days the meetings had been focused on buying a fish tank and some fish. Residents and staff had been researching what fish were suitable, the costs and how it was going to be financed, and it had got to the point when a decision was to be made. There was a long discussion about where the tank would be sited and who would be responsible for cleaning it and feeding the fish. Everything was considered and agreed, and everyone at the meeting approved the wording of the record in the meeting book. Within a week the tank had been set up and the fish were put in. The residents each adopted a fish, which they named.

The week after the fish had settled into their new home, there was an inspection. The inspector had returned to check whether The Willows had complied with the three standards (choice, activities and food) found non-compliant at the last inspection. Gill had rejigged the paperwork to meet the inspector's requirements and he was happy with the result. He enjoyed his visits to The Willows and was uncomfortable with having to insist on compliance with some standards that he knew were irrelevant to the way The Willows operated. Sometimes he wished that he could work in such a stimulating and creative environment instead of being compelled to pick fault with a place that was so obviously good for the people who lived there. The residents were always so friendly and quick to welcome him and show him round, and this was one of the signs of just how good The Willows was and how much they were involved in making it good.

Just as the inspector was about to go, one of the residents asked him if he'd seen the new fish tank. He was taken to see it and told all about it. He was duly impressed, but as he prepared to leave for the second time, he hesitated and wondered if a risk assessment had been completed for the tank. What if there was an accident? What if the tank got smashed or a resident drank the water or ate the fish food? What if the electrics went wrong? What if…? He had seen the tank and he hadn't checked the risk assessment. It was just the sort of thing his manager would ask him when he put it in his draft report.

Very reluctantly, the inspector asked Gill if he could see the risk assessment for the fish tank. There wasn't one or, at least, there wasn't one that was acceptable to the regulator. Of course, all the risks had been fully discussed at a series of community meetings and there was a record of those, if he'd like to read the book.

In order not to put herself to any more trouble and to keep the home compliant, Gill agreed to write the risk assessment and fax it to the inspector, and he would not report that there was no risk assessment. It took Gill only half an hour; she was used to doing them.

Specialisation, labelling and role definition

Due to endless technocratic attempts to bring certainty to social care (including social work) and to create procedures to fix problems, care has fractured into specialisms and specialists, into clients who are categorised by age, mental and physical frailty, dementia, mobility, illness and condition, etc. Services specialise in similar ways but principally are divided into care homes with and without nursing, dementia or non-dementia, learning disabilities (often referred to as LD), substance abuse, mental health, etc. And then within services, such as care homes, there are specialised units. Nearly all of this specialisation is dictated by the system rather than by the clients.

Specialisation commands higher fees, so a person with some form of dementia could be living very happily in a small family-run care home and be paying half what she would pay if she were to be diagnosed with dementia and be sent to live very unhappily incarcerated in a big specialised dementia care home with nursing. Likewise her good friend the domestic worker (who knows all about her and communicates brilliantly) in the small home is considered to be unskilled and untrained whereas the dementia specialist nurse in the large care home, who gives her pills, dresses her leg ulcer and has no conversation with her whatsoever, is highly trained and comparatively well paid. Too often specialisation focuses on the service and its personnel and not on the client. The client must adapt to the specialism rather than the service drawing on its special knowledge, skills and experience to respond to the client's individual needs. The institutional defence of specialisation makes it possible for the specialist dementia nurse working on the dementia unit in the specialist dementia nursing home to treat the leg ulcer, administer the medication and never to engage person to person with the client.

Office work

Care workers and managers escaping from the core task to the office and the elevation of office work and administration above care work are both defences against the anxieties inherent in caring. There is a seemingly inexorable demand for paper and computer work that results from the supposed power and authority of the 'head office' and of all those organisations that govern a care service from outside and 'above'. These external managers, regulators and 'governors' are office-, computer- and paper-based operations; they don't give care. Yet feeding them with paperwork is regarded as a priority. It's noticeable in care homes that the administrator (or clerk) is often seen as higher up the pecking order than a senior member of the care staff, a team leader for example. And then it's common to find that the team leader prioritises sitting at a computer or hangs around the office in order to establish their status. If you see it from the client's or care worker's point of view, it will be obvious how absurd this is.

Increasingly managers work 'office hours', yet nine to five Monday to Friday is less than a quarter of the working week of a care home, so it might be appropriate for a manager to spend just ten hours a week on office work and 30 hours with staff and residents where the real work gets done.

Such is the power of outside bodies that your care service survives only by feeding their hunger for paperwork. Your own success and survival as a manager are measured by office work, and if you are to find the time to spend with clients and staff you will have to pass some of the paperwork on to them! This has to be challenged at source rather than colluded with. We are faced with a situation in which the most difficult and stressful direct work is left to the lowest paid employees and the relatively easy work (the paperwork) is done by managers operating as highly paid clerks, and usually not doing it very well. Management and leadership are not the same as clerical work.

Compliance

'Compliance carries with it a sense of futility for the individual and is associated with the idea that nothing matters and that life is not worth living.' Donald Winnicott was writing about children in *Playing and Reality*, but the deadening – and abusive – effect of imposing compliance can be seen in adults as well.

Compliance, bullying and abuse, and the projection of guilt (scapegoating and blame) are linked psychological processes. The public are asked to believe that we can eliminate abuse by demanding tighter compliance of all care providers and punishing the persistently non-compliant. While the exposure and punishment of non-compliant providers assuage guilt, at the same time they perpetuate abuse.

The propensity to bully is built in to command-and-control organisations. Schools, the police and armed forces, prisons and care homes are thought of as likely breeding grounds for bullying and abuse, but such tyrannies are rife in many other workplaces such as newspapers, offices, the civil service, and in the compliance regime of regulators.

Targets are set, delivery is demanded and failure is punished, and all the system learns is how to cheat to meet the targets. And it is passed down the line…to the inspectors, to the providers, to the managers, to the staff, and, yes, to the residents of care homes and the clients of domiciliary care.

The clients of your service are quite likely to be 'non-compliant' people. Their need for social care means that in some way or ways they are unusual and disadvantaged. Therefore, imposing any regime of compliance is punitive and institutionalising, and could manifest itself in bullying and the suppression of residents' sense of self.

Avoidance

In services that care for people who are dying we might expect staff to avoid getting too close to or too fond of clients because the repeated experience of death and loss, of grief and mourning could be so emotionally stressful. Yet for these organisations to give good care, staff must make close, loving relationships and feel genuine loss when someone they care for – and about – dies. It is one of the most difficult parts of the work – to face death, to feel loss and to grieve.

Of course, we all avoid – consciously and unconsciously – unpleasant and difficult people, issues, events and feelings. We can avoid talking of such things, we can be ill or elsewhere, we can 'forget' or find something more urgent has called us away, we can be 'unavoidably' late.

Avoidance can take the form of distraction. So, in a team meeting, someone jokes or passes sweets around at just the moment when a difficult issue is staring everyone in the face. Or, at that point, someone rushes out to the toilet, or chooses to answer the phone. An irrelevant but 'hot' subject is substituted for the difficult one that no one will talk about.

Collusion

Collusion is often linked to avoidance. We collude with avoidance, when we should challenge it and question it. Informally, every member of staff is complaining about how unpleasant and difficult a resident is and yet, when the time comes to talk about feelings in the team meeting, this resident isn't mentioned. Collusion is of course a group process; you cannot collude if there is no one to collude with. We 'go along with' something, we don't challenge, we don't question. We can tacitly agree that 'this isn't the time to talk about this', and then it doesn't get talked about. It takes great courage and commitment to break a collusion, to put oneself outside the group consensus.

Collusion is also linked with scapegoating. It is a group 'agreement' or turning a blind eye. This person (the scapegoat) will carry the responsibility and blame for the rest of us.

The group hug: To squeeze the discomfort out of the group

In social care work we must be aware of each other's feelings and should talk about them. However, because of the stressful nature of the job, we tend to rush in with sympathy in an attempt to rescue all (including ourselves) from facing up to hard truths. Bereavement and sickness elicit the expression of much sympathy, but what is not admitted, faced or expressed is that a colleague's absence means greater strain on others and may mean letting down clients. Where does the anger and resentment go? What about the envy that is engendered by the attention a colleague receives?

When such difficult issues are discussed directly between people in a team meeting, and someone goes out of the room crying, three or four others leap up and follow them to console them. It is easy to sit around or even huddle together with arms around one another saying what a great team we are, but the same sort of group commitment to hammering out disagreement and acknowledging ill-feeling is more important but much less common.

It's fashionable for organisations and teams to make much of celebrating success. Cakes are bought, certificates are awarded and photos are taken. There's a prize for the employee of the month, and bonuses and vouchers are handed out in recognition of individual and team achievements. This is a manifestation of a glitzy culture, a 'because you're worth it' self-centred superficiality that serves to hide and suppress rather than work with the harsh realities of social care. It is patronising and manipulative.

In a team whose work is essentially with loss and vulnerability, such lightweight, fleeting and showy responses to difficulty and success discourage thought, reflection and learning while encouraging superficial sentimentality, obedience and conformity.

Regional and national awards competitions and events have multiplied in recent years. What began as a celebration of good work and recognition of essential staff who had previously been ignored, has turned into a plethora of commercial opportunities for sponsorship and self-congratulation by all those organisations that are making money out of care. Amidst the glitz and razzmatazz, the real work and the serious issues of social care are lost while the great and the good of 'the sector' hand out awards to emotional winners who have to go back the next day to face what care is all about. Just as a staff team get together at Christmas, get drunk and hug each other in a desperate attempt to reassure themselves that it's not so bad after all, so the care 'industry' spends a fortune on such opportunities to parade their good intentions and admiration for those who generate the profits for their companies. Every aspect of behaviour at every level in social care calls into question what lies beneath the surface of this extravagant facade.

Information and guidance overload

It is neither desirable nor possible to absorb all the information and guidance that is produced for managers of social care.

What is going on when legislation, guidance, regulation and standards, spawning further elaboration and guidance by the 'improvement agencies', proliferates to the extent that nobody, even if they devoted their whole working life to doing so, could possibly absorb and learn it all?

Very little of it is new. The principles of social care and the components of leading it are no different now than they were 40 years ago. In the 1980s the principles were expounded in several seminal publications such as *A Positive Choice, Home Life* and *Homes Are for Living In* (see 'Books and Other Resources'). These were then recycled and, often, distorted and misrepresented through the allied movements of standards and inspection, quality auditing and a new qualification regime, all of them more concerned with the surface procedures of care than with understanding what was beneath the surface. This superficial approach to social care was encouraged by the idea that the work could be ordered, packaged and delivered, and that getting care right was a matter of effective procedures.

The approach remains dominant and has been reiterated and reinforced every time it has been painfully and publicly shown to be ineffective. Rather than, as in this book, starting with the core task, understanding care as a psychosocial system within wider systems, and acknowledging the importance of working with the feelings that are always present beneath the surface, government and policy makers redouble their failed efforts to command and control good care, and fail again. At the time of writing, the government is encouraging all care organisations to sign up to a so-called 'Social Care Compact'.

There are specialists, trainers and consultants in every aspect of care, and they are keen that you, as manager, are made to feel that it is essential to engage them or to attend courses and conferences laid on by them. Usually, they are specialists in their own subject, or they have prepared a course that they will 'deliver' (for a price), or they are peddling a new product. In reality, many know little about how their particular speciality fits in with the whole system of your service, and they are unlikely to have had direct experience of leading a service such as yours. However, they will promise much in terms of compliance and quality, handing out their own certificates to show that your service has achieved whatever quality mark they are selling.

Such quick fixes are 'packages' which are ordered, paid for and put on show. Nearly all terms used seek to deny vulnerability and dependence, and all procedures are designed as shortcuts to good care. They work at a superficial level but do not engage with all that lies beneath the surface of care.

WORKING WITH WHAT IS BENEATH THE SURFACE: CREATING THE THERAPEUTIC FRAMEWORK TO ENABLE YOUR STAFF TO WORK WITH LOSS, FRAILTY AND DEATH

As the manager of this service, you lead the way in working with what is beneath the surface so that your team can work at a feelings level with their clients. Care workers need a framework of support and learning which will equip and maintain them emotionally for the work. They need to understand themselves, to understand the feelings of their clients and to understand the feelings that are engendered by their care relationship with their clients. And, of course, you have to lead the way by doing the same for yourself and with them.

In order to reduce institutional defences, you build a framework that can contain the emotional stress and disturbance (anxiety) which is part of the work. You create this framework through formal and informal, individual and group supervision, teaching and regular meetings in which feelings are discussed alongside and as part of everyday work issues (such as handover meetings).

ESTABLISHING A THERAPEUTIC FOUNDATION AND FRAMEWORK

More will be said about designing and enacting this framework in Chapter 5. In this chapter we are considering why the components of the framework are necessary to attend to what is beneath the surface.

GITA DESIGNS A STAFF SUPPORT
STRUCTURE AT THE LIMES

Within days of starting her immersion in the work of the home (by working shifts with all the staff), Gita had begun to design and build a new staff structure. As with the residents, she took directions from what she could see staff needed. They were working under intolerable stress, compelled to ignore residents' needs as they worked to a routine of personal care – dressing, washing, bathing, toileting, changing, bed-making, laying tables, serving meals, running activities, writing notes and taking breaks. Meanwhile, others were going through similar routines at other levels – medication rounds, dressings, turning, catheter care, pressure areas, care records, and cooking, washing up, laundry, cleaning, mopping, disinfecting, and…breaks. Staff were allocated to a 'floor' or group of residents but it changed from day to day. The handovers were from the nurse in charge of one shift to the one in charge of the next. If, as often happened, a shift leader was working a 'long shift' (7a.m.–9p.m.) there was no handover in the middle of the day.

From the first day, Gita witnessed the distress of the staff. Some showed it all too obviously, crying and looking miserable. Others tried to hide it behind cynicism and detachment. And others were angry. The conversations at breaks were accounts of the extremes of soiling that had to be dealt with, or complaints about working conditions and pay. The staff room where these conversations took place was dirty and uncomfortable. There were old, defaced notices and memos from head office on the board alongside press cuttings about abuse in care homes.

On her third day, Gita started handover meetings with all the staff when the late shift came on duty. She asked every member of staff to say something about one resident they had worked with on the shift and one thing about how they were feeling. She started and then she went round the room. Less than half were able to say anything about how they were feeling other than 'I'm fine' or 'OK'. Gita did this at every handover opportunity that she had and she asked her senior staff team to do the same. She then asked the housekeeping staff to come to handovers. Several times, her deputy and team leaders said they couldn't be there because they were too busy or had an important phone call. Gita said they must be there, the handovers must take place and they must start on time and finish on time. Once, during a handover, the administrator came in and told Gita that Sarah (the company's managing director) was on the phone for her. Gita said that she was in a handover and she would ring her back after it had finished.

In the second week Gita called a full staff meeting and told all staff who were off duty on that day that they would be paid for attending. There would be a full staff meeting every fortnight and all staff, including housekeeping, maintenance and catering would be rostered on for the meeting. She chaired the first two meetings and then insisted that chairing would be taken in turns. Supervision and staff training were scheduled for the same day. Head office were informed that no outside calls would be taken during the meetings.

Out of this initial structure of staff support grew the next stage of design. The staff started to work in integrated teams with smaller groups of residents, which in turn became group living units or households. Each household had its own team of nurses, care staff and housekeepers, and each team had a leader. Each household operated as an autonomous unit within the overall community. Gita trained all the households' team leaders in supervision by supervising them, and everyone working at The Limes was expected to have supervision at least once a month.

Households had a team meeting once a fortnight and the whole community (The Limes) had a big meeting bringing all the units together in the weeks that the household teams weren't meeting on their own. Later on there was a monthly community meeting of everyone in the home and the relatives, friends and volunteers.

It was far from easy to design and build this structure. When staff have been without support and have had no opportunity to talk about their feelings, about their clients and about their own needs (such as training and thinking about their own career development) it is very difficult to begin because it's painful, unfamiliar and scary. But because Gita knew this, she was not discouraged by the initial resistance and resentment. The staff had to trust her first, to see that she was serious and wasn't going to leave them exposed and unsupported. Gita could lead these great changes because she was attending to what was going on beneath the surface, and knew that if she didn't begin by working at that level, any attempt to reorganise and transform the care would not succeed in the long run.

Being there

It's essential for a leader of therapeutic work to be there when and where the work is done, and sometimes to expose yourself to the work. You will not be believable or trusted unless your staff see that you have done, can and will do the real work that you are asking them to do.

When you are starting from a very low base, where the standard of care is poor and staff are struggling to get even basic physical care completed, meetings, supervision and training will not work unless you have directly experienced (and are seen to experience) the apparent hopelessness of the task. If your staff are facing seemingly impossible dilemmas, such as insufficient time to do the job properly, you will grow in authenticity in their sight and understand for yourself what needs to be done. This is not only to demonstrate to your team that you can roll up your sleeves and get your hands dirty, it is so that *you* can learn from *your* experience, that you can feel, think and find meaning in your feelings. Your plans for change will be forged in the heat of real feelings and grounded in practicality, and will thereby stand a much better chance of success.

Regular team meetings

In a good care home, there are likely to be handover meetings three times a day, from one shift to another – early, late and night duties. In a day centre, a beginning and end-of-day meeting is useful. With dispersed staff teams such as home care, it is much more difficult and time consuming to get people together, but workers do need to meet regularly for support, learning and development, and if they can work in small teams and arrange and run their own meetings, this will produce excellent results for clients.

Big, whole-team or service meetings are important for all social care organisations to keep everyone working together with a sense of direction and progress. This is much easier to arrange in care homes than it is in a home care service, but it is needed in all settings.

Supervision

Every contact you have with members of your team, individually and together, has a supervisory element to it. You are their manager: everything you feel, think, say and do is of interest to them. And the reverse is also true: you need to give the same sort of attention to them. This is a supervisory relationship and it continues even when you are not with your supervisee. Much of it is beneath the surface. For example, your physical presence or absence is usually known, but even when you are not there, the service, the clients and your team are 'in mind' – they in your mind and you in theirs.

If we accept that much of this work (social care) takes place 'beneath the surface', the word *super*vision – as in *over* vision or *above* vision – might imply that the process and relationship is not concerned with what is beneath the surface. However, in this case, we can think of the word as meaning an overall view that sees connections between many apparently different areas. An aerial view of terrain can reveal many things that are simply not apparent at ground level, not only connections but subterranean (beneath the surface) features and differences. So imagine supervision to be the opportunity to survey, analyse and reflect on the work. By creating a supervision framework, you build capacity in your service for everyone to be fully engaged with a client *and* to be able to think about what's going on around them and beneath the surface (see 'Relaxing and flexing boundaries to meet clients' needs' in Chapter 4).

At its most familiar, supervision is, of course, those regular one-to-one sessions between supervisor and supervisee, when the supervisee talks about, reviews, reflects on and thinks about their work, themselves and their feelings, and plans and learns. The role of the supervisor is to listen, guide and support, and to encourage the growth of self-development and learning in the supervisee. This will be done by speaking less than the supervisee, by waiting before jumping in and advising, and by inviting the supervisee to take an overview in order to be able to see the whole landscape and what's beneath the surface.

In these planned, one-to-one supervision meetings, the fundamentals of supervision are established, and from that base the process becomes part of the work culture. There are brief supervisory exchanges: stand back, listen, reflect, think, go back in. Supervision is carried with staff into their direct work, into handovers and reviews, into staff meetings and coffee breaks. The process is internalised to the extent that people who are well supervised can use it even when they are on their own, like a broadcaster having an earpiece with a supervisory voice helping by giving an observation, angle or suggestion. It becomes part of the work culture and is renewed, regenerated and passed on every time it happens. Supervision is essential for everyone who is working with feelings and relationships – social carers.

Training and staff development

There are practical areas of the work that everyone must know about and be competent at: safety, fire, moving and handling, medication, food hygiene, infection control, etc. The training should be part of induction and refreshed regularly. The practice learned in such training should be taken very seriously on the job, otherwise the honesty and authenticity of the work is undermined. A disconnection between what is taught and what is practised is damaging to the work culture and may be harmful for clients. As manager, it's useful to teach such courses and to take part as a learner, and show your team that you can and do practise what you preach. For example, the misuse of 'personal protective equipment' (gloves, aprons, etc.) is common. As manager, you need to know when and when not to use such equipment, to understand why staff are misusing it and to show them how to use it. All such practical training has underlying meaning and anxieties attached to it. These are life and death issues; they are about being in close contact with disease and contamination; they are frightening and they remind staff of the massive responsibilities that confront them.

In addition to the practical mandatory training (above) the best training and development is on the job, in supervision, handovers, team meetings and training events that you, as manager, put on using your own resources in the service and commissioning trainers to come in. Really good social care services are places of training and professional development. While external qualifying and other training is essential, and those on external courses have an obligation to share their learning in their workplace, it is in the application of training that the real learning and development grow. Factual knowledge, theory and ideas must be discussed, tried out and applied. Thus, your service becomes a place in which to be trained, a place of learning and development, where staff will be proud to say they learned. Take in students on placement, open the service to universities and colleges, create a culture of learning and ideas, but beware of the academic tendency to disconnect professional qualification and advancement from the core task, and from the feelings and anxieties that trigger the lofty academic defence of detached observation and analysis.

Daily life and special events

I have described and discussed the structure and framework (meetings, supervision and training) designed so that staff can work with what is going on beneath the surface, but it is from the daily life of the service that your clients draw their care and support. The structure of daily life and the framework of care and support enable your clients to live their lives: some just coping, some recovering, some moving on, some contributing, some happier and healthier, some enabled to live or die better. So, in designing the structure and framework of daily life (and this would of course be with clients' participation), you work with what is going on beneath the surface.

Frequent and regular social occasions, such as mealtimes in a care home or preparing a meal in someone's own home, have meaning far deeper than their surface; in the case of meals far deeper than the mere nutritional value of the food. You design mealtimes so that they can connect at a social and emotional level. Creating a familiar way of greeting someone when going into their room or flat as a care worker connects people at a deeper level than wishing a stranger 'good morning' in the street.

So the fabric of everyday life in social care must be carefully woven to work at a deep emotional level as well as at a practical level.

At the beginning of this chapter, I wrote about the need for containment and holding, and that a social care service should act as a container for the feelings and anxieties of the staff and clients, and can hold people whose lives are threatened, chaotic or falling apart in the way that a mother can hold a baby safely and securely. Everyone at some times in their lives – and always as a baby – needs containment of feelings and emotional – and sometimes physical – holding. And I use the idea of the *woven fabric* of everyday life as a suitable analogy for the capacity of social care to hold and contain.

The routines of everyday living are part of the fabric: strong but flexible to accommodate a variety of needs and forming a pattern to reflect the variety of people. Different people will make their mark on the pattern and will become a part of the whole. To continue with the woven fabric analogy, the routines are the warp and the individual threads that go to make the pattern are the weft. The strength of the warp carries the variety of the weft.

In addition to the everyday routines, there are special events such as birthdays and wakes, entertainments, retirement and leaving parties (and welcoming parties), festivals and commemorations. All have their overt purpose and their deep significance. It is just as important to mark a death as a birthday, perhaps more so. In a care home, for example, deaths are frequent but that should not make them commonplace. Everyone has important dates and anniversaries in their lives, and sometimes no one else knows. A home care worker might find a client is thoughtful or tearful with no immediately apparent reason. Through sensitive, quiet and reassuring listening, the worker discovers that it is the birthday of a long dead sibling or spouse, or an anniversary, or something – and it may not be the date – has brought painfully to mind a stillborn child or some such tragedy. Equally, making a special effort for a birthday or religious festival touches deep feelings and associations.

SOME QUESTIONS AND ACTIVITIES TO CONSIDER, DISCUSS AND USE IN ACTION LEARNING SETS

- What do your clients bring with them to your social care service?

- What feelings does your service manage to contain?

- What feelings does your service fight off or find ways of defending itself against? See Figure 3.1.

- What are the losses that your clients experience?

- Why is there a need for the 'containment' of feelings?

- Consider the story 'Containing panic at The Hub'. Has anything like this happened to you or your service, and how did you manage it?

- What effect does the fear and denial of dependency and vulnerability have on your service and on social care more widely? Try to identify specific instances.

- How are anxieties successfully contained in your service?

- Think about the individual, group and institutional processes, the feelings, defences and unconscious processes beneath the surface in your organisation. See Figure 3.2.

- Consider the story 'Identifying and dismantling defences at The Limes'. Can you see yourself thinking and acting in the way that Gita did? What would happen if you did?

- Think about the following anti-task processes and defences in the wider system. Are they all negative or can you find merit in some of them?

    - 'Putting procedures in place'

    - Denial

    - Personalisation

    - Risk aversion

    - Specialisation, labelling and role definition

    - Office work

    - Compliance

    - Avoidance

    - Collusion

    - The group hug

    - Information and guidance overload.

- Think about the story 'A failure to assess risk at The Willows'. What would you have done in Gill's place?

- How do you or would you like to create a therapeutic framework to enable your staff to work with loss, frailty and death?

- Think about the continuation of Gita's story, 'Gita designs a staff support structure at The Limes'. Do you think this approach would work in your service?

- Discuss some of the main features of establishing a therapeutic foundation and framework:

  - Being there

  - Regular team meetings

  - Supervision

  - Training and staff development

  - Daily life and special events.

- Consider if and how each of the sections in this chapter applies to your service.

4

BOUNDARY

WHERE YOUR SERVICE INTERACTS WITH ITS ENVIRONMENT (OUTSIDE IT) AND THE USES OF BOUNDARIES IN LEADING CARE

We have looked at the context – the environment – of a care service, what it does (its core task) and what is going on beneath the surface. Now we look at how it is defined by its boundary and how that boundary is both the demarcation line and the meeting line: the point of connection and transaction between the organisation and its environment.

THE CONCEPT OF BOUNDARY

It is essential to understand the concept of individual and organisational boundaries when considering your clients' choices and decision-making, and your and your staff team's roles, responsibilities and accountability.

When you say to a member of staff, 'It's your job to…' you are defining the extent of a role and its responsibilities, and making that member of staff accountable. When you say to a care home resident, 'This is your room…' you are implying to them that they are in charge of the boundary of their room, because if it really is *their* room, they make the decisions about who and what cross the boundary. They may also delegate some decision-making as in, 'Please don't knock on my door in the morning. Just come straight in, pull the curtains back, and wake me with a nice cup of tea.' Boundaries play a constant, crucial role in all care services.

For every job and role there is an area of responsibility and accountability defined by a boundary. However, it is often poorly defined, and unclear boundaries create confusion and conflict. As a manager of a care service, you should be able to lead the core task within a defined sphere, and it should be clear who makes which decisions. People (staff and clients) come in and out of your area of management, and it is your job to decide if and when they come in and go out. You should decide on staff selection and on the acceptance of clients to your service. Sometimes you may have to decide on staff dismissal and on ending a client's use of your service. You are also responsible for the relationships, collaboration, integration, negotiations…all the 'transactions' with other services, organisations, across and beyond the boundary of your service.

In larger organisations, the boundaries of your management may be broken by the operation of centralised offices and sections such as human resources (HR), finance, 'quality assurance', marketing, and often by your own line managers who can undermine your authority and muddle accountability by making decisions that belong with you (see 'The core task is the whole task' in Chapter 2). Similarly, in small organisations, proprietors may blunder into the areas that they have appointed you to manage and interfere in decisions that they have employed you to make.

WHAT DOES BOUNDARY MEAN?

A common modern meaning of the word 'boundary' is a disciplining limitation on behaviour, usually of children and young people. It's also used in the sense of personal boundaries, as in the limits and defence of personal space. The use as a systems term is similar; it means the line of demarcation around a system as in a boundary fence or wall. The physical demarcation of an area – garden, yard or building – is a common enough reality for all of us, as is the boundary of a town, region or country that has no physical marking apart from roadside signs to indicate that you are entering or leaving an area with an unmarked boundary.

The rope marking the edge of a cricket field is a further example of a boundary. It doesn't stop anyone or anything crossing it; indeed, much of the game of cricket depends on the players and the ball crossing or not crossing the boundary. The game takes place only within the boundary; once the ball is outside the boundary it is 'dead'. To continue just a little further with the cricket analogy: there is no set area for a cricket field, and some boundaries are bigger than others. In addition, the boundary is the subject of discussion and dispute: did the fielder make the catch within – and not touching – the boundary? Was it a 'four' or a 'six' (both 'boundaries')? The issue is whether or not the ball cleared the boundary without touching the ground inside it (a 'six'). The game takes place within the boundary but much of it is conducted across the boundary (batters coming 'in' and 'out'), scoring 'fours' and 'sixes'. Spectators are not part of the game and must stay outside the boundary. The team coach and the ground administrators and managers must also keep out while the game is played.

There are of course electronic and digital boundaries. We now think in terms of firewalls, passwords and keys that take us in and out across a boundary. So, boundary is a common and useful concept and word, and it is especially useful when thinking about systems of social care.

The idea of the care service as a 'container' in the previous chapter also leads us to consider the concept of the boundary holding or containing the organisation and differentiating it from its environment. Where does it start and end? How is it defined? To a large extent we identify people, living beings and non-organic objects by their exteriors, by their boundaries. While we are aware that a human or an animal has an inside, it is the outside that we see, recognise and touch. It is by the covering (of skin, clothes, hair, scales) that we identify living beings, and it is this covering and the openings in it that both contain the living being and conduct its transactions with its environment, in and out and across or through its boundary. In organisational terms we should concern ourselves as much with the boundary and what takes place (what is 'transacted') between the inside and outside of the organisation as with what is going on beneath the surface.

All living things have a boundary and interact with their environment. There would be no interaction – and therefore no life – if the boundary itself was not permeable both ways, so that the living thing could 'import' (take in), process and then 'export' (put out) whatever is needed to sustain life. Our skin is permeable. We breathe in, extract oxygen from the air and breathe out. We eat and drink, we process nutrients, we use energy and we excrete waste. Teams, companies, organisations also take in, process and export, and all this is done across the boundary, within the boundary and then back out across the boundary again.

Our clients' views of our services are initially formed at the point where they first experience them at a boundary. For example, the client may first meet our organisation during the initial assessment of their needs and at the forming of a contract for care. The assessment may be being conducted in the client's own home. The person who is making the assessment represents their care service and literally crosses the client's boundary (their front door). The client may never have heard of the organisation and so may have only general preconceptions or prejudices combined with the actual experience to go on. In this instance, that initial meeting – the meeting at the boundary – will be critical to how the subsequent care relationship develops. Similarly, the client may come to the service, also to make an assessment, and crosses the service's boundary to do so. The boundary and who is in control of it do make a difference to the power relationship.

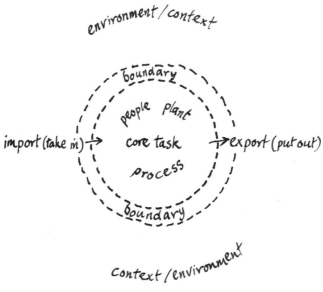

FIGURE 4.1 BOUNDARY

In addition to the transactions across the boundary, there are the transitions – moving from one place (actual and figurative) to another, from one state of being to another. When someone moves from living in their own home to living in a care home, we refer to and think of this as a transition. A transition implies a change…a threat and a loss as well as a change for the better. When a resident of a care home dies, there is a transition from life to death (often referred to as 'passing', or 'passing over' or 'away'), and the dead body is removed from the building, out across the boundary again.

BOUNDARY DECISIONS ARE 'KEY' DECISIONS

Entries and exits, and all sorts of transactions across the boundary of your organisation, relationships with other organisations and with the environment outside the boundary, are where many key decisions are made. Keys open and close boundaries…doors and gates. The boundary is the line that defines the extent of your responsibility and accountability.

As manager, you should be the leading decision-maker at the boundary: decisions about who and what comes in and out, and how you work with all outside people and organisations. You should be responsible for deciding who works in your service (staff selection) and whom the service supports and cares for. You manage a team or service which is defined by its boundary. Of course, you may share or delegate these decisions but they should be yours to make.

ENTRIES

Who and what enters your service – selecting and appointing staff, and assessing and accepting clients are the most crucial decisions.

In some organisations, the boundary decision of who enters the service as a client is already determined by the core task. For example, a service that has been set up to care for people in a defined situation ('reablement', specific medical conditions and categories, specific circumstances) may accept every- and anyone who comes along up to the limit of available places. However, there will still be key decisions to make about the capability and capacity of the service to care for some clients, and this may involve the manager refusing admission to clients whom the provider organisation considers suitable.

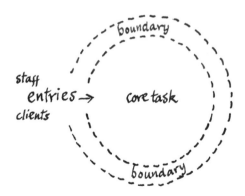

FIGURE 4.2 ENTRIES

STAFF SELECTION AND APPOINTMENT

It is all too common in larger organisations, especially when there is an established 'human resources' (HR) department or section, to find that decisions on the appointment of staff have been taken away from the manager of the service where they are going to work. The process of identifying a vacancy, recruiting and appointing have become a 'head office' function, and HR staff have thrown themselves into the process with understandable enthusiasm. It will come as a shock, and may initially be seen as simply being difficult, when you say that you will take these key decisions. Of course, you will need the help and full cooperation of HR, but the decisions should be yours.

STAFF RECRUITMENT AND SELECTION AT THE LIMES

At The Limes, the activity organiser is leaving, having done an excellent job by making her role redundant. Everybody is now an activity organiser, so Gita considers sharing out the 20 hours a week allocated to the post amongst all the staff, thereby recognising and paying for some of the many voluntary hours the staff have been giving to support all sorts of activities and events in the home. On the other hand, Gita wonders if that would be a mistake because this generous voluntary spirit is now part of the home's culture and paying for some of those hours might discriminate unfairly; indeed volunteers who are not members of staff might feel that they should be paid. For example, Martha might be upset because she comes in every Thursday morning as a volunteer to run her very successful singing group. So Gita decides to wait before advertising.

Gita consults widely amongst staff, residents and relatives, and comes to the conclusion that the most pressing need is for someone to do the laundry at weekends. No one in HR can possibly have the experience, knowledge and understanding to make this decision, nor could they advertise for and select the weekend laundry person, because they have insufficient grasp of the crucial importance of the role and how it's performed. However, they can – and should – do all the admin work. Gita sends the bare bones of the job description and specification to them; they write them both and return them for approval. They then advertise where Gita recommends. With her full-time laundry person and someone from HR, Gita shortlists and then selects. The panel, led by Gita, decides who is the right person, and HR again do the essential administrative work to make the appointment. (Staff selection panels at The Limes now include a resident who has attended recruitment and selection training.)

It has taken much effort and negotiation with the head office, but now at The Limes, selecting and appointing new staff is a boundary decision that is made by the manager or is delegated. However competent and well motivated, people outside the boundary should not make key staffing decisions for inside the boundary.

CLIENT ASSESSMENT, ACCEPTANCE AND COMMITMENT

As the manager of your service, you are the 'key' decision-maker when it comes to deciding who you can, should and will support. This can be seen in terms of opening and entering 'doors', whether it's the client's own door to their house or flat that your service will go through, or the door to your service (such as a care home or day centre) that they will come in through. And this 'key' decision is literally the key to the door – a boundary decision. Of course, you may delegate this decision.

ACCEPTING A NEW CLIENT AT 4CS

Let us look at the decision that Gloria made at 4Cs three years ago when Mrs Smith was first referred by the local authority for 'brief' visits.

This was at the time when 4Cs was in its infancy as a home care cooperative. They were desperate for referrals from the local authority, and felt that they had to take on whoever was referred in order to get established and to build a good working relationship with the council commissioners (Careshire). (Gloria and her colleagues had made a considered decision to allow the boundary of 4Cs to be softer and more permeable than they intended it would be in the long run. In the future there would be times when 4Cs hardened and partially closed their boundary in order to protect the organisation at times of change.)

Gloria took a call from adult social services giving Mrs Smith's circumstances. She had recently come out of hospital after an emergency admission with a severe urinary tract infection, and needed only 'checking' on. There might be a little bit of tidying and reminding to eat and drink, and very simple food preparation. Mrs Smith was diabetic but managed her own medication and was 'self-caring'. The brief visits were to be three times a week in the afternoon. This referral had come originally from the district nurse, via the GP practice, to adult services. Adult services had not yet assessed Mrs Smith and so they were passing on details that had already been through two care organisations. Although Mrs Smith's circumstances were by no means life threatening, it was urgent to make an assessment and to 'put a care plan in place'. Gloria was well aware that this was in the nature of a risk reduction exercise (or 'arse covering', as Gloria rather more robustly put it to her colleagues) for the chain of referring bodies. She also realised that the real risks for Mrs Smith were being passed on to 4Cs.

Gloria immediately phoned Mrs Smith, made an appointment and left the office that afternoon to visit.

RECOGNISING AND RESPECTING
THE CLIENT'S BOUNDARIES

Mrs Smith was very cautious at the door, and it took Gloria some time to persuade her that she should let her in. But, once in, Gloria was welcomed and Mrs Smith made them both tea, and a new packet of diabetic biscuits was opened. The old lady apologised that there was no cake. She was at pains to explain that since coming out of hospital she had felt too weak to bake. In any case, she added sadly, who would eat the cake? Her family were far off and most of her friends had died.

Without writing a note, Gloria gathered (and remembered for later when she would complete her written assessment) a great deal of information about her new client. Had Gloria asked her a list of questions from an assessment form and written down the answers, Mrs Smith would have told her that she could manage in every way and really didn't need support. As so often happens, the referral, initially made by the district nurse who visited Mrs Smith when she returned home from hospital, passed on by the GP surgery, and then passed on again by adult services, was made to reduce the risk of something going wrong and blame being attached to each of the referring agencies. A minimum of 45 minutes of 'care' a week in three visits would effectively reduce the risk to the referring agencies and pass it on to 4Cs.

EXPORTING RISK ACROSS BOUNDARIES

Managing primarily for risk reduction is linked to 'failure demand', the demands on an organisation created by the failure to do the right thing in the first place (see 'Failure demand: The noose that strangles initiative and leadership' in Chapter 6). Instead of focusing on the core task – Mrs Smith's needs and care – care organisations (in this case community nursing, GPs and adult social services) focus on the risks that Mrs Smith's needs and care pose to them. So, by passing on Mrs Smith's care needs to 4Cs, who at this stage of their development can't say no, and by allocating inadequate resources to meet those needs, the referring organisations are building in the likelihood of failure, but at the same time reducing the risk to themselves. If, as is likely, the care is inadequate, the time and resources consumed to investigate and establish blame – failure demand – will probably exceed the resources that would have been needed to do the job properly in the first place. The reality has been the exact opposite of professed policies from government downwards, where it was proclaimed over many years that preventative support, keeping people out of hospital and long term care, was a central aim of health and social care.

COMMITMENT

Gloria knew that it was not feasible to meet Mrs Smith's needs in three brief visits a week. She was lonely and becoming increasingly confused and forgetful. It took Mrs Smith a quarter of an hour to make a cup of tea, so by the time she'd done so the carer would have left. However, Gloria had told Mrs Smith that the district nurse, her doctor and social services were all concerned and had asked 4Cs to 'pop in' three times a week to check she was OK. As Gloria put it, 'It'll help everyone to stop worrying about you,' and Mrs Smith was never one to refuse to help other people.

'Will you be coming, Gloria? I'd look forward to that; we get on so well.'

'No, Mrs Smith, it won't be me, but I will come with whoever it's going to be on the first visit. I've now got to go back to social services to get the agreement from them to start our visits. And, very likely, someone from social services will come to speak with you before we start.'

It wasn't Gloria's job to sort out who was going to pay. Whoever was going to pay for these brief visits, 4Cs would lose out financially in the short run. A brief visit to check someone was OK was expected to take at least 15 minutes and was paid for as half an hour. Having visited and – almost inevitably – implied a commitment to Mrs Smith, Gloria wasn't about to turn round to her and say they couldn't possibly do it for the paltry sum of money on offer. Although Careshire paid a slightly higher hourly rate than two neighbouring local authorities, it still fell short of the minimum fees calculated by the national home care trade association based on a mere 3 per cent profit margin.

BLURRING THE BOUNDARIES OF RESPONSIBILITY

Gloria returned to the 4Cs office and immediately emailed her assessment to adult services, giving a very clear summary of Mrs Smith's circumstances and needs. In her view, Mrs Smith needed a half-hour visit every day, including weekends, because she was lonely and isolated, and very confused and forgetful. The likelihood of recurrent self-neglect, and especially of not eating and drinking, leading to further emergency admissions to hospital, was high. Mrs Smith was also extremely anxious about the state of her flat, and kept saying how untidy it was and how it needed a proper spring clean, although, as far as Gloria could see, it looked very clean and tidy. It was clear to Gloria that short daily visits with enough time to chat, to check that Mrs Smith was eating and drinking, and taking her medication, and give a little practical help if needed, would be the best way to prevent, or at least postpone, the need for another emergency admission to hospital and going into a care home. Gloria also thought that even just a day a week at The Hub lunch club would be a good idea.

THE EFFECT ON MRS SMITH OF
BREAKING HER BOUNDARIES

The adult services worker went to assess Mrs Smith. She had to make a financial assessment, and armed with Gloria's professional social care needs assessment, an adult services care planning assessment would be drawn up. Mrs Smith found the experience very difficult. First, the assessment officer had to ask her many questions about her finances – her pension, benefits and other income, outgoings, and even about her savings (which Mrs Smith felt was none of her business). She also wanted to know all about her family, daily habits, neighbours, her medication, what she ate and drank, and so on. The woman even asked if she could look in the bathroom, bedroom and in her fridge. It felt so intrusive and, although she'd made tea and got out the biscuits again, she couldn't wait until this woman left the flat. When asked about how she was managing, Mrs Smith assured her assessor that she was perfectly fine and needed nothing.

Within a couple of days, Mrs Smith experienced Gloria's friendly and helpful visit followed by the social worker's intrusion into her home and life. She had again become confused and anxious. She felt as if she'd done something wrong and that other people had invaded and were taking over her life. She didn't feel as if she was in charge.

LINKING THE USE OR MISUSE OF
BOUNDARIES TO THE CORE TASK

However individually well intentioned the social services worker was in her visit and assessment, she was currently working for an organisation whose task had become the rationing of resources. It spent much time and concentration on excluding (keeping outside its boundaries) the very people it was set up to support, and weighing that objective against the risks to the organisation posed by each potential client. The social worker spoke to her of a 'personalised care plan', but the effect on Mrs Smith was oppressive and frightening. In contrast, Gloria had been friendly, polite and respectful. Mrs Smith felt she was still in charge of her flat and her life. They had such a pleasant conversation, and she had happily told Gloria all about her life, yet by the time the social worker had left, Mrs Smith was agonising about losing her flat, being 'put in a home', losing her savings (a few thousand pounds deposited in the Post Office for her funeral), and having more people barging into her home to 'keep an eye on her'.

Mrs Smith is only one of hundreds in Careshire. Having satisfied herself that Mrs Smith was not going to die if allocated as little as 45 minutes a week of home care, that the client had food and fluids available and that, by her own admission, she didn't need support, the social worker told Gloria that the contract for care was to be as previously suggested:

three afternoon visits a week (Mondays, Wednesdays and Fridays) of a minimum of 15 minutes each to check that Mrs Smith was eating and drinking, taking her medication and was OK. The contract would run for four weeks and would be reviewed after three.

EXITS

Having control over who and what leaves your service, most significantly staff and clients leaving, is just as important as who and what enters.

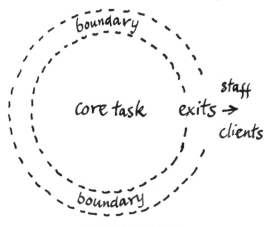

FIGURE 4.3 EXITS

Evidently, a service working at full capacity should not accept more clients without a corresponding 'exit' of people. When working with older people, a good proportion of this export will take place because people die and thereby create vacancies for new clients. In addition, people move on: they may move to use other care services or they may no longer need support, and sometimes it may be necessary to move them on. Staff also move on: some retire, some resign, and a very few may need to be dismissed.

While some of these 'exit' decisions are hardly decisions at all because, like someone dying, events dictate the outcome, there are problematic boundary decisions to be made when the manager has to tell a client or member of staff to leave. These are inevitably difficult decisions but, like 'entry' decisions, they should be made by the manager or whoever the manager has delegated to make them.

GILL ASKS A CLIENT TO LEAVE THE WILLOWS

Edwin has lived at The Willows for three years. He's 43 and works at The Hub. For his first year, he refused to leave the house, but gradually staff and other resident members of the household got him out for short walks in the village, to the GPs' and dentists' surgery and, by stages, for bus trips into Careborough and into work. Edwin is now well known in the village and has a position of responsibility at The Hub. Until Martha came to The Willows two months ago, Edwin was settled, happy and fulfilled.

Martha is 22. She's a talented singer and can play the piano by ear. Her ambition is to be on a TV talent or reality show. Her childhood and adult history of abuse have left her confused and disturbed, vulnerable to sexual exploitation but also yearning to fall in love. Having made a casual but untrue allegation about having a relationship with a male member of staff (see 'Investigating an allegation at The Willows' in Chapter 2), she has fixed on Edwin as the object of her love and desire.

Edwin has never had a sexual relationship. He is flattered but unnerved by Martha's insistent attention. Martha's initial therapeutic plan was thrown off course by the intervention of her social worker who instigated a safeguarding investigation when Martha made the allegation. This meant that the community as a whole were inhibited in their contact and relationship with Martha, and instead of being able to ignore or to gently confront and challenge Martha's sexual attention, Karl and other men on the staff had to avoid her. That in turn undermined and confused the residents who became unusually reticent, and it irritated the whole staff team who were not used to having the way they worked knocked off task by outsiders. Professional boundaries had been broken by the interference of external workers.

Maintaining a balance between Martha's and Edwin's rights and freedoms and their protection and care was proving difficult. The whole household – residents and workers – was affected and by no means united in their attitudes. Most of the other residents strongly disapproved and felt that Martha should never have been accepted at the home. Their settled community was scandalised and in turmoil. The situation challenged the whole basis of the therapeutic community.

Gill, as manager, leads the community in a way that supports the power of the residents to take responsibility for themselves and each other and, with the help of the staff, to run the community themselves. However, she recognises that in order for a therapeutic community to survive at The Willows, she has to retain a veto over key boundary decisions, such as the entry and exit of residents and staff. The whole community is formally involved with the selection of staff and the acceptance of residents, and their experience and views are certainly taken into account when Gill makes decisions on people having to leave the community, but Gill is responsible and accountable for the decision.

The regional charity that owns and runs The Willows is also influential in these boundary decisions, sometimes exerting pressure on Gill to admit residents when they are not suitable, and on one occasion to accept a member of staff from another home, who was also not suitable. The charity, through its group manager, is always reluctant to clarify the boundary of Gill's management responsibility in spite of Gill's insistence that if she does not have this key decision-making power, she cannot lead effectively. And it is at crucial moments such as this (whether Martha was to stay or go) that the boundary issue is tested both internally, with the staff and residents, and externally with the voluntary organisation that runs The Willows.

In this instance, the outcome was that Gill – very reluctantly – asked Martha to leave because, although she fully expected the longer-term therapeutic plan for Martha to work for her, she could not rely on the professional partnership with her social worker and wasn't willing to risk Edwin's health and happiness. Of course, finding an alternative placement involved collaborative work, but Martha's departure also created long discussions, reactions, splits and reverberations in the community that continued for many weeks afterwards. As the leader of good care at The Willows, Gill had to hold the community together (see 'Uncontained feelings and the need for containment' in Chapter 3), to help everyone to learn and grow through this traumatic time.

Having found himself isolated by his attachment to Martha and deeply upset by her leaving, Edwin spends a lot of time alone in his room. He gradually re-establishes his place and relationships within the community, goes back to work and begins a relationship with Jean, a colleague at The Hub who lives (with support from 4Cs) in her own flat.

REINSTATING A BROKEN BOUNDARY

All aspects of The Willows' boundary had been tested and damaged by this episode. While Gill would still argue that Martha's original admission and her therapeutic plan were right for her, the social worker failed to respect and use the boundary properly. She did not provide full information, she allowed herself to blur the boundary between her own political and moral outrage at Martha's sexual exploitation and her duty as a professional partner in enacting the agreed therapeutic plan, and she attempted to interfere in decisions that were not hers to make.

Martha's social worker was not the only culprit in breaking The Willows' boundaries: Gill's regional manager, put under some pressure from the social worker's team manager to keep Martha and very reluctant to create a vacancy and drop in fee income, told Gill that Martha should stay and that it was both unjust to Martha and poor professional practice to insist that she left.

Even though half her team, Edwin and two more residents and nearly everyone outside the home was telling her she was wrong, Gill stuck to her decision. She was the only one in a position to make it. She had to weigh up the probable consequences for Edwin and Martha, for the other residents and the staff team, and for the whole community. She had to use her judgement. Of course she had doubts about it and did everything she could to find a suitable placement for Martha and to make her leaving as positive as it could be. In doing this she attempted to rebuild a working relationship with Martha's social worker and she used her good connections and collaboration with other local services.

During this troubled episode, as manager of The Willows, Gill had to use the boundary to hold the community together and to protect it from intrusion from outside. Her 'parenting/containing' role was called on to give stability and care even though several members of the 'family' didn't agree with her decision. The community – staff and residents – felt threatened by the possibility that Gill's manager (representing the overall organisation (charity) that ran The Willows) and the social worker and her manager (representing the local authority) would somehow 'take over' the home and destroy the community. Gill had to convey a sense of safety and continuity in the face of a growing sense of insecurity and anger, even though she felt the same. She knew that there would be pressure put on her to accept a new resident quickly and that she would have to handle that boundary decision carefully, balancing the conflicting arguments inside and outside the boundary, trying neither to use the boundary in too defensive a way nor to open it prematurely.

PARTNERSHIPS AND COLLABORATION

Your service works across the boundary with volunteers, informal and unpaid carers, family and friends, and with other people and organisations. Successful partnerships and inter-organisational collaboration depend on the positive use and clear definition of boundaries. To work together well, it's essential to decide who does what and who is both responsible and accountable for what. The more agencies that are involved in social care, the more effort has to be put in to collaborate and to maintain boundaries. The old adage that good fences make good neighbours is relevant here. Much good neighbourliness is fostered leaning chatting on the fence, and long-standing good neighbours sometimes put a gate in their adjoining fence so that they can water each other's gardens, pick the produce and feed the chickens while their neighbours are away. But such arrangements can turn sour quickly if either side is too casual and forgets the importance of the boundary.

FIGURE 4.4 PARTNERSHIPS AND COLLABORATION

COLLABORATIVE WORKING PAYS OFF FOR MRS SMITH

It is true that in accepting the referral of Mrs Smith for home care in the first place (knowing the mismatch of commitment and reward on offer), Gloria was influenced by the need to establish 4Cs as a willing, responsive and reliable home care agency, but this did not reduce her clarity about the organisation's core task and her awareness of the boundaries of her service and the boundaries of her clients' lives and homes. However, the core task of Careshire's adult social care service had been reduced to rationing. Social workers could not effectively collaborate with 4Cs (or any other care services) while their first consideration when faced with a referral for care was not, 'How can we help with the resources we've got?' but, 'How can we preserve the resources we've got by excluding all those potential clients whose needs if unmet will not damage our organisation?' (misuse of the boundary). It is very difficult for two or more organisations to collaborate successfully with such different approaches to need.

Nevertheless, Gloria's approach was so positive that she was able to set up collaborative work with other organisations and to bypass the local authority's negative influences and even transform them (see also Chapters 6 and 7).

4Cs is a cooperative and the permanent members work for and own the organisation. They have a longer-term and broader view of their role and the role of their organisation than most employees do. Many established members (worker/owners) previously worked for social services (when the local authority directly employed home care staff) or for private home care companies. In joining 4Cs they committed themselves to a different ethos and way of working. They are treated fairly, they own the organisation and make the big decisions together, they are united by and committed to the core task of home care and can organise their own work in small self-managing teams. They are known and respected in their community.

All this means that 4Cs is an organisation that connects the community it is rooted in and, like The Hub, invites, stimulates and encourages partnership working and collaboration. In addition, Gloria and her senior colleagues in 4Cs are leading members of the Careshire Social Care Managers' Network (see Chapters 6 and 7).

So when 4Cs take on a new client, even at the early stage of development when they took on Mrs Smith, they not only think about the care they will provide, but they start actively seeking to create a support network by their collaboration and partnerships with other care providers and social support groups. These connections are made at a 'street' level, with neighbours and shops for example, and at a professional level, with colleagues in other organisations. The Hub is a great resource – as it is intended to be – for accessing information and support.

When eventually Mrs Smith goes to live at The Limes, she already knows the home and some of the staff. She has been to events there and she has even stayed there for three nights while her flat was being decorated by The Hub Caps, a young volunteer group based at The Hub (see below, 'Mrs Smith and the Hub Caps'). Because of the collaboration between managers and their services, Mrs Smith was also a regular user of The Hub, going to the lunch club twice a week and, incidentally, being a pal of Edwin, who did a great job of keeping The Hub grounds tidy. Careshire Adult Services financed her home care and her short stay at The Limes before then funding Mrs Smith's long-term care there, but the local authority would not have been able to create the network of support that began with 4Cs and then grew to take Mrs Smith through the last years of her life. (Mrs Smith died at The Limes five years after she'd first been referred by Careshire Adult Social Care Services.)

EXTERNAL RELATIONSHIPS AND REPUTATION

Your service depends on building and maintaining good external relationships and an excellent reputation, both with other social care organisations and teams, and with the public.

It seems like a long time ago that local authorities' welfare departments and, later, generic social services departments ran 'home help' services for elderly and disabled people who needed some housekeeping help to enable them to remain in their own homes. Generally, 'home helps' had a list of clients that they went to regularly and, with a relatively small number of exceptions, the home help service was very well regarded and well liked. Many home helps were friends and neighbours, and were a very strong part of the community. Day centres and lunch clubs were also part of the fabric of non-residential care, although they did have a tendency towards institutional care. Care homes had the mixed reputation that they now have – some good, some mediocre and some very poor – but those that were seen as 'local' homes, as part of their neighbourhood (and they may have been private, voluntary or local authority) were highly valued.

FIGURE 4.5 EXTERNAL RELATIONSHIPS AND REPUTATION

With the many changes in legislation, regulation and funding over the last 20 or more years, social care has, unsurprisingly, changed and is probably less local and less community based. Local authorities have been – to some extent – forced to cut the funding of care to all but those in most urgent need. They have pared down the fees they pay to care homes and withdrawn funding from voluntary organisations that are not actually contracted to them to provide services. The result is that most local authority adult care has become little more than a gatekeeper to limit access to social care and, with some honourable exceptions, they are seen and experienced as unhelpful, begrudging and officious.

However, given the demise of local authority social care, there are many opportunities for care organisations – those run for profit and not for profit – to fill the gap and to create local community care networks. Local authorities can certainly help with this through their commissioning practices, by enthusiastic support and participation, and by freeing up some of their remaining facilities.

MRS SMITH AND THE HUB CAPS

While Mrs Smith's way of life in her own flat was being satisfactorily supported by 4Cs and her twice-weekly attendance at The Hub Club (luncheon club and day centre), Gloria, Geoff, Gita and Jean (Edwin's girl friend who was a volunteer at The Hub Club) arranged with her to have her living room decorated by The Hub Caps.

The Hub Caps were a group of young people who volunteered as a mini community task force, a sort of roving working party who could put their hands to almost any practical job. For a decorating weekend, they would be led by a professional decorator, and were usually in and out within 24 hours. The Hub Caps were a social group as well as a work group, and they included a broad mixture of young people from colleges, school leavers, some in their first jobs and some unemployed. Jean was trying to persuade Edwin to join but he said he was too tired by his job by the end of the week and he sometimes had to go in at weekends. The Hub Caps wore distinctive yellow baseball caps with HC on the front – except they usually wore them back to front.

Jean suggested the decorating project to Mrs Smith whose first thought was where would she go while the decorators were in. So Jean talked to Geoff, who talked to Gloria, who talked to Gita and it was all arranged. Mrs Smith, usually so protective about her flat and so concerned about her boundaries, accepted the arrangement because she knew everyone and trusted them. It all went well. She enjoyed her brief stay at The Limes and was delighted with her newly decorated living room. Immense care had been taken to put everything back exactly where it was before.

When she felt her boundaries were broken by strangers and when she didn't know what was happening, things went wrong for Mrs Smith, and she got frightened and wouldn't let anyone help. The key to Mrs Smith's good care was collaboration across well-maintained boundaries.

Social care managers (heads of care homes, home care and day care, for example) working together and at the boundary between the service they manage, other organisations and the community, have it in their power to transform local social care. If the experience of the public and of social care clients is that all these services, despite their varied management and ownership, work together to one end, the result of such collaboration will be greatly enhanced reputation and trust (see Chapter 6).

A good reputation is important for all social care providers. When care homes and home care organisations give an excellent service, and when it is evident that they work with each other in collaboration rather than against each other in competition, the word gets around and there is no better means of promoting the service. There are so many ways in which organisations can collaborate, but to do so they must be clear about their different core tasks and boundaries. Establishing and maintaining a good reputation is led by the manager with a generous and open 'can do' ethos, taking every opportunity to support and collaborate with other care services and groups.

THE USE OF BOUNDARIES
MRS SMITH'S BOUNDARY ISSUES AT THE LIMES

Three years after Mrs Smith was first supported by 4Cs, she came to live at The Limes. She had a room on the first floor overlooking the garden. She was a fastidious woman; she liked her room to be clean and tidy. Physically very frail, she was losing her memory and was frequently confused as to her whereabouts. She had been going to the lunch club at The Hub twice a week and staying the whole day. Mrs Smith came to The Limes because she was no longer able to cope at home. Her flat had become unhygienic because she had stopped allowing her 'home help' (supplied by 4Cs) to enter, and she had become dangerously malnourished. Her family lived a long way away, and between them they could manage only fortnightly visits.

Mrs Smith benefited from the good food and company at The Limes; however, she began to stay in her room for most of the day because she suspected that while she was out, people were going in without her permission. When she first arrived, after being helped to get up and get dressed, she would put on her coat, leave her room and 'go out' to spend the day in the communal areas of the home, as if she was going to the club. She always checked that her room was locked when she left it, and she wore the key on a string around her neck.

At about 10.30 each weekday morning, Ellen, the housekeeper, went to find Mrs Smith, who might be in the sitting room reading the paper or chatting to friends, in the kitchen preparing vegetables or baking, or downstairs in the main lounge at some communal event or entertainment. Ellen would ask her for her room key so that she could do a 'quick tidy up'. To begin with Mrs Smith was quite happy about this. It had been discussed fully before she came to the home. In fact it was a great relief to her to know that her room and bathroom would be kept nicely. She got to know Ellen and trusted her. They invented a little ritual of handing over the key and returning it, and had struck up a close friendship.

THE BOUNDARY OF ELLEN'S JOB

As the housekeeper for the household (group-living unit) where Mrs Smith lives, Ellen is an integral part of the care team, and housekeeping is an integral part of the care. She is the lead person for all things domestic and homely. She works from 7.30a.m. to 3.30p.m. on weekdays and sometimes does a 'care' shift in the evening or at weekends. She is there for the handover meetings in the morning and the afternoon. At the Limes, everyone has their role and responsibilities but this doesn't mean that no one else does housekeeping: everyone does it, including the residents. Ellen leads housekeeping; it is her main job and, although it is integrated with the work of the whole unit team it has a boundary, so when there are decisions to be made about a new vacuum cleaner, furniture, decoration, the arrangement of the dining room... Ellen takes the lead.

Although Mrs Smith needs some help with 'personal care', mainly with washing and dressing, she is most concerned, most anxious and potentially most reassured by the state of her room and bathroom. If her room is secure, clean and tidy, Mrs Smith can enjoy life. This is why it was decided that Ellen would be the most suitable person to be Mrs Smith's keyworker and, certainly, if you asked Mrs Smith to whom she was most closely connected in the home, she would choose Ellen.

So, as with other keyworkers and in addition to her lead housekeeper boundary, Ellen has another boundary around the support and care that Mrs Smith needs. If Mrs Smith's room gets in a state, she goes to pieces. And when her room is untidy she won't let anyone in. This is what happened with her flat.

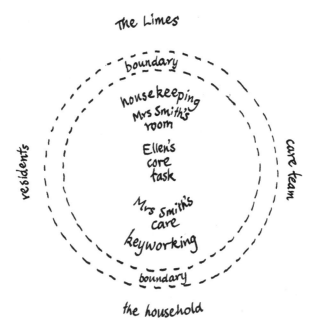

FIGURE 4.6 THE BOUNDARY OF ELLEN'S JOB

Mrs Smith's problem started when Ellen went abroad on holiday for two weeks. Although Ellen and other staff had told her and reminded her about the holiday, and Ellen sent her a picture postcard, it came as a shock when a man (in fact a fairly familiar member of the 'bank' staff) approached her when she was having coffee with friends, and asked for her room key.

'What are you wanting with my key? I don't know you. Ellen does my room, not you.'

A couple of minutes later, Mrs Smith was asking urgently to be helped back to her room, and there she stayed.

She refused to let anyone in. Two days later she was persuaded to come out for lunch while the bank staff went in to clean and tidy, but in the process familiar things were moved into slightly unfamiliar positions. When Mrs Smith returned, she was aghast and said she'd been burgled. Although the room was now in a better state, Mrs Smith refused to leave. She had her meals brought to her but she'd lost her appetite and they were often left untouched.

RELAXING AND FLEXING BOUNDARIES TO MEET CLIENTS' NEEDS

When Ellen returned from holiday, Mrs Smith took a couple of days to allow her back into her life. She had felt Ellen's absence as a desertion but couldn't identify what it was that she had lost. The postcard had helped to remind her, but the shock of being asked for her room key by a 'strange' man threw her into panic. However, soon everything seemed back to normal and Mrs Smith resumed her accustomed way of life. Nevertheless, Ellen and the team could see that they needed to make some adjustments in the way boundaries were drawn and managed to enable Mrs Smith to tolerate Ellen's absence. In creating such firm boundaries in the interests of establishing a secure relationship and respecting Mrs Smith's fierce demarcation and defence of her room boundary, they had created a problem. Because it all seemed to work so well, they hadn't risked helping her to build on the security that she had established to become more open and flexible about her room boundary. When they looked at Mrs Smith's range of friends and secure relationships in the home, they realised that she was perfectly capable of being adaptable and easy-going, and the well-intentioned and initially necessary insistence on an exclusive relationship with Ellen had now become counterproductive.

Using her next supervision session, Ellen met with her team leader to discuss the way forward. They came up with the idea of making a gradual transfer of keyworker to introduce Mrs Smith to another close relationship. They knew that the way to Mrs Smith's heart was the cleaning of her room, but the person they had in mind, Grace, was recently employed as a care worker not a housekeeper.

Mrs Smith had taken a shine to Grace when she first came because she seemed like a younger version of Gloria (4Cs), who had made such an impression on her more than three years previously. Like Gloria, Grace was Nigerian or, more accurately, her parents were Nigerian and she was born in Careborough. It was less Grace's looks that reminded her of Gloria and more her voice, manner and presence. She had the same reassuring attentiveness and a lovely laugh. So when Ellen began to take Grace with her when she went to wake Mrs Smith in the morning, it was more than acceptable for the old lady to allow her into her 'domain'.

This transfer of keyworker progressed smoothly, at first with Ellen and Grace sharing equally and then Grace gradually taking on the main keyworker role. Ellen and Grace would try to avoid being away at the same time, but Mrs Smith's anxieties had reduced and her sense of security had increased to the extent that she could now tolerate different people coming into her room.

However, there was a wider adjustment of roles and boundaries of which this move was an early and influential example. Gita had been talking with the whole staff team about the limits put on roles, responsibilities and relationships by the job descriptions of the company. At The Limes, ever since Gita had worked with everyone and done every job in the place in her first three months, the formal limitations of job descriptions had been stretched and blurred. While boundaries in relation to the place and care relationships were changing, expanding and adapting to suit residents' needs (e.g. Ellen and Grace), there was a tension with the formal job descriptions and the pay scales that went with them. (It would be wrong to think that this flexing of boundaries left them vague. In practice, boundaries were constantly being redefined, so that, although they were changing, they were agreed and understood within the service, but not yet in the company as a whole.)

It was a lot to ask of Ellen to take so much responsibility and to act as a keyworker, when she was still being paid at the housekeeper's (domestic worker) rate. Similarly, it was a lot to ask of Grace to do what to an outsider seemed like simple domestic work (cleaning Mrs Smith's room) when she was a graduate, being paid as a care worker and thinking of a future in social care management. Gita renegotiated all the job descriptions at The Limes so that housekeepers, like Ellen, and care workers, like Grace, had a much broader remit and were paid on the same scales. Effectively it raised the housekeeper role from a 'domestic' to a 'care' role to integrate all aspects of care in the core task.

SUGGESTIONS FOR EXERCISES, DISCUSSION POINTS, GROUP WORK

- Sketch a diagram or picture of the service you manage showing its boundary. What's inside and what's outside?

- Consider the transactions – the comings and goings, the negotiations and collaborations – that take place across the boundary.

- Which of these is problematic? Accepting clients? Moving clients on? Selecting staff? Moving staff on?

- Consider in particular your dealings with your manager/ proprietor. Are they making your decisions?

- Consider your own dealings with the people you manage. Are you making their decisions?

- To what extent do your existing job descriptions limit the potential of your staff? Is there anything you can do about this?

- Consider the boundaries and decisions of the people who use your service, your clients. Are you making their decisions for them or are you supporting them to take their own? And what is the connection between your responses to the first five points and to this one? (Remember the core task of your service.)

5

MANAGER AS LEADER

As manager you are the leader of professional practice, the guardian of values and principles, and you put the care and wellbeing of your clients above all other considerations.

Taking on the leadership of a social care service is a weighty responsibility, the contemplation of which can reduce you to adopting an attitude and position of cautious compliance that will inevitably undermine your capacity to lead. Yes, you may be able to manage to get by, to maintain a level of functioning that is acceptable to those who appointed you and those who regulate you, but you won't be doing a lot for the people who need the service you manage (more on this in Chapter 7).

As leader, you are out there in front. You are known and you are followed. You encourage others to lead and you support them with your leadership.

This chapter takes an alternative look – sideways and beneath the surface – at a range of everyday issues that you deal with as a manager, encouraging you to question, to think for yourself and find a way through, to trust your own authority and thereby to grow from mere management to leadership. If you are a social care manager, it isn't possible to make the radical changes that you are seeking overnight; you have to keep the service running and, to do so, you have to live and work with the overall context as it is now. As you will have already discovered, this book is about those radical changes. For practical advice now and links to the appropriate legislation and guidance, go to *The Social Care Manager's Handbook*, which is updated annually. The subjects of this chapter parallel most of the sections of the handbook.

LEAD WITH VALUES AND PRINCIPLES: BELIEVE IN WHAT YOU ARE DOING

You can't lead social care if your heart's not in it. You came into this work because you believed that, at some times in our lives, we all need help and support from others that is more than can be given by family and friends, and therefore we need a social care system. (If that is not at least part of your motivation, you may be in the wrong job.) It is, by nature and definition, a communal (social and shared) resource. While the informal and unpaid support of family, neighbours and friends provides the bulk of care, there are times and circumstances when more is needed and this is the social care that you lead. So, first, a social care service is founded on a belief in and commitment to supporting those who need help, and accepting that this is a shared, communal responsibility.

You and those whom you lead must be able to empathise: to have the imagination to understand how other people are feeling, and to act accordingly. Along with empathy go compassion and respect: to have the sensitivity to feel concern provoked by another's pain, loss or upset, and to continue to regard and treat that person as an equal human being, deserving dignity and kindness.

As a manager, you have been given power and responsibility. Even if you feel that your power is very limited because you are expected to obey orders and follow procedures, those whom you manage will regard you as having power over them. And, even if you feel that your responsibilities are overwhelming and wide-ranging, that you are held accountable for many areas of the work where your power to act is impossibly constrained, you will still be regarded as responsible by your employers and the outside bodies to whom you are accountable. To lead social care, you need authority. You take and earn authority when you combine power and responsibility. It takes courage to take authority.

The act of taking authority (and stepping up to leadership, see Chapter 7) requires you to use your imagination (how things could be), creativity (building a better system), responsive adaptation (being light on your feet) and the courage to take a step in the dark (act even though the effect of your action is uncertain). Further core values underpin the authority of a good leader: fair- and open-mindedness, justice, equality, human rights, commitment and hard work.

However, these principles and values are a sham without integrity. Integrity (wholeness) binds them together in one. You must be honest and reliable through and through. You have to earn the trust of your team. Your values, principles and motivation must shine through all you do and will be tested repeatedly to make sure that they are authentic. Nobody's perfect, so when you lapse – as we all do occasionally – acknowledge, apologise and put it right or put it back together again without delay.

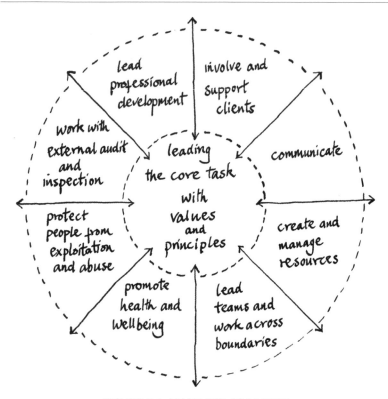

FIGURE 5.1 MANAGER AS LEADER

LEADING THE CORE TASK

The essential, guiding position of the core task has been explored in Chapter 2. You, as the leader of good care (the core task), are responsible for keeping it in that central position at all times. Many pressures, conscious and unconscious (see Chapter 3), will conspire to divert you and your service from the core task.

When someone needs your service, they or the person speaking on their behalf, or commissioning the care from you, should be clear about what they want from your service and why this will improve their situation. For example, if someone can no longer manage some of the ordinary, basic actions of everyday living – getting up, bathing, preparing food, laundry, cleaning, and so on – having these things done for or with them will enable them to enjoy doing some of the things that make their life interesting and worth living. So the request for help (and the subsequent care plan) should make clear what the objective of the care is. Such a plan is positive and has as its objective improvements and enhancements to the person's life, and these become the core task. Help with getting up is not an end in itself; it enables the client to go out, to socialise, to visit a friend, to watch the birds on the bird table, or to go and have breakfast and sit and snooze in front of the telly before lunch if that's what they want to do. Help with getting up in the morning is no help at all, if there's nothing to get up for.

The alternative, so-called 'deficit' model of care is focused only on what the person cannot do and what has to be done for them. So the work becomes an endless round of mundane and purposeless tasks with no good reason to do them apart from maintaining a person physically – fed and watered, cleaned and clothed. Without the positive objective of enabling someone to live their own life (and to die) as well as possible, the physical maintenance routines and procedures tend to break down.

Those who commission care may be doing so because they need to prevent neglect, and they fail to think and plan beyond an immediate objective of heading off the possibility of failing to 'safeguard'. With cases of self-neglect, it can happen that someone is moved to a care home with a plan for physical care – say nutrition – yet if there is no plan beyond physical care, all that has been achieved is moving the location of continuing self-neglect to a service that will be held responsible if the problem is not 'fixed'.

A common scenario, in which the core task of care is put to one side, is moving a 'wanderer' (someone who puts themselves in danger by leaving their home and forgetting where they are) into a care home with the intention that they will be kept safe by being prevented from leaving on their own. Effectively, the referrer (social worker or family) is asking for them to be incarcerated, which is illegal, unethical, and is not the core task of a care home, yet it happens all the time.

This illustrates the importance of clarifying the objectives of care, and for you, as leader of the core task, not to allow your service to be used for other purposes. It takes considerable courage and determination to resist the pressures from outside, and to stick to the core task, but when managers join forces and refuse to collude with what amounts to poor practice, it has a powerful effect to improve social care.

Thirty years ago, when I was head of a very large local authority care home which was designated as the 'emergency/short-term' home, I refused to accept referrals that were purely to do with housing or accommodation. Inadequate housing was tolerated because care homes were being used for housing. Social workers had to justify a placement on the grounds of social care, not accommodation on its own. I was very unpopular in the social services directorate but the effect was to clarify our core task and to force social workers to clarify theirs.

Domiciliary (home) care is usually an individual, couple or family care service, whereas care homes and day care services have a substantial and important component of group care. The recent, largely positive, emphasis on 'personalisation' has wrongly implied that all social care provision is individual.

Personalisation has been a movement to put the client in charge of their care, whether they pay directly for it (direct payments and self-funded care) or not. And although governments have enthusiastically promoted personalisation, their motivation for doing so is mixed between the laudable objective of clients designing, commissioning and controlling their own support systems, and of saving money, cutting jobs and breaking up the potential for collective action amongst clients and workers. Personalisation is an individualistic approach to care.

As a care leader, you will concentrate solely on providing the best care, which is most likely to be a combination of individual and collective and communal. Why do people like going to a lunch club or a day centre? Mostly because of the other people there: they go for the company and group activity. Such social facilities have been considerably reduced in number as local authorities have withdrawn funds because generally they are not seen to be compatible or effective as part of the 'personalisation agenda'.

MRS SMITH AND THE HUB CLUB

Ever since The Hub opened there has been a seven-day-a-week midday meal available in the cafe. Many formal and informal groups meet before or after lunch and use the cafe for lunch. On one side of the kitchen there is a self-service counter and till, and on the other there is a hatch opening onto a large public room that can be hired for events and clubs. Amongst the clubs is the day centre and luncheon club run by a local charity with two full-time workers and a team of volunteers (one of whom is Jean). This is known as The Hub Club. The local authority provides transport and paid a daily fee for some of the people – mainly older people – who attended the club.

The catering is run by a local bakery, which had opened their own cafe next to their shop and then took on the cafe at The Hub. The food at the cafe was subsidised to the extent that there was no rent charged on the premises and no charges for energy, so the meals were cheap.

When Mrs Smith first had brief support visits from 4Cs three days a week, Gloria arranged with social services that she could attend The Hub

Club two days a week. This worked very well, apart from some difficulties with the transport not turning up on time or not turning up at all.

After Mrs Smith had been going to the club for about a year and getting her home visit three days a week, under pressure of central government cuts the council decided to cut funding to day centres and lunch clubs, and to The Hub. Such provision was considered to be very old fashioned and institutionalising and against the spirit of the new 'personalisation agenda'. The council's own social services transport was also due for closure and the drivers all went on strike.

Mrs Smith had made good friends at the club and the regular pattern of her care suited her well, but her life began to disintegrate again when the club closed. It was opened again within two months by the volunteer team, but the transport was not reinstated and Mrs Smith was, by this time, refusing to let anyone into her flat to help. (This led to her move into The Limes.)

INVOLVE AND SUPPORT CLIENTS IN RUNNING AND EVALUATING THE SERVICE

As already noted above, policy initiatives or 'agendas' such as personalisation have mixed motivations and mixed results. The main stated purpose of the policy is to put people who use a care service in control of their own care, thereby fitting services to users rather than users having to fit in with services. Allied with this purpose is seeing the client as an individual customer or a consumer buying bespoke services that are 'packaged' and 'delivered'. In theory, if you choose and buy services in this way, price and quality would match supply and demand, and the 'market' of care services would be self-adjusting and self-regulating. However, while there are customers who can choose and pay for precisely the services that they want, and change suppliers if they are dissatisfied with what is 'delivered', the majority of social care users are not in this position even if they pay for their own care. The dominant position of suppliers has not been broken by personalisation, and services frequently fall short of the standards that 'customers' have a right to expect. The widespread failure of care services to meet commonly expected standards has caused governments to set out standards in law and regulate services to protect consumers. One effect of this has been to bureaucratise care, to take control away from consumers and, arguably, to make providers more accountable to external demands and audit than to the people who use their services. To remain in business, providers have to keep their 'accounts' (records, policies, procedures, etc.) in ways that are acceptable to the auditor or regulator. As in other businesses, the accounts do not necessarily reflect the reality on the ground and the experience of service users.

While the negative sides of personalisation and regulation are fighting it out, as the leader of your service, you can pursue an alternative approach that is integral to the core task by getting your clients directly involved in running and evaluating the (their) service.

Clients running and evaluating their own services

First, a word of caution: not all of your clients will want to be involved, and others may only do so when they've had the time to gauge the authenticity of the offer and feel it's worth the effort. Some people, understandably, will argue that they are paying for a service that you have a responsibility to manage and evaluate.

Care services have different cultures and that provides some choice for clients. For example, at one extreme there are care homes that are run like four or five star hotels. Such 'care hotels' have smartly dressed staff in uniforms who must treat 'guests' with due deference. Here customers do not expect to have any sort of close relationship with staff who stay discreetly in the background. Surprisingly, quite a few care companies aspire to such provision, and some do it better than others. The target clientele are wealthy people who can afford to buy 'luxury care' but are often disappointed because the reality doesn't live up to the hype, and because, as they need more care, they discover that good care cannot simply be bought and supplied; good care comes with mutually respectful and appreciative relationships.

In contrast with the 'care hotels', services that have care relationships at their core are by nature democratic and participative organisations. Even if there is never a formal residents' meeting, a small, family-style care home may effectively meet at least once a day at the main mealtime. There may be eight people, including two care workers, sitting around a large table. Issues are discussed and decisions made. Likes, dislikes and opinions are aired. Plans are formed; the day is remembered and commented on. When something significant is agreed, one of the company may write it down in the book that's kept on the sideboard, and different workers will read it the next day.

In a larger place, this process of feedback, discussion, evaluation and decision-making is formalised. There is a residents' meeting or a community meeting. It is chaired and minuted so that everyone gets a fair chance to make their views known and business is got through in the time available. This is the group or communal side of involving clients in the running and evaluation of the home. Both the formal and informal involvement and participation require leadership from the manager, which then spreads and is handed on to and through the whole community.

Home care clients need to be able to give feedback and evaluation in different ways, and to feel that their views and ideas are taken into account, not only in their own care, but in the way the home care organisation is run. For example, a lack of continuity of carers will be a problem for most clients, and this should be picked up by the management, not only for that client but as a general problem for all clients, and action must be taken. As the leader of home care, you must find a way, or several ways, of inviting feedback and proving to your clients that you have listened and it makes a difference.

Individual feedback and involvement are also important where there is a strong communal and democratic culture. Some clients would prefer to give their opinion in private and others need skilled help to gather their thoughts and communicate their point of view. Again, the leadership and culture established and passed on by the manager will spread through the organisation.

'Quality assurance'

Much is made of 'quality assurance' processes, both internal and external. Many large providers have a department and a director of 'quality'. Even the regulator 'quality assures' its own work, testing it for consistency, which tends to result in reports that are full of stock sentences and standard evaluations, making it very difficult to discern any differences between one 'compliant' service and another. Several 'quality assurance' and 'star rating' schemes have been adopted by care provider associations and companies, all aimed ostensibly at 'driving up quality', but more probably making services more adept at answering questions correctly, marketing themselves and convincing regulators that they deserve to be rated as 'outstanding' or 'excellent' or whatever the 'quality' word of the moment is. It is hard for most care organisations to resist the lure of 'quality', but the whole concept is regressive and, rather than encouraging innovation and the lively participation of people who are using your service, it restricts, standardises and coerces compliance. It also diverts time and energy that should be applied to the core task. 'Quality assurance' is essentially packaging: a commercial and marketing concept, wasteful of resources, superficially attractive but disappointingly empty.

4CS' FEEDBACK FROM CLIENTS

Gloria is a realist. She knows that she has to produce some sort of 'quality assurance' evidence for regulators and commissioners, so she designs it to be useful and authentic.

When 4Cs first started, she had to get 'customer feedback' in order to get customers! So she designed the simplest of forms for her clients to fill in – and their families, visitors and other professionals – and every client had a care notebook with numbered pages, that stayed with the client and to which anyone could contribute comments. All the ways of contacting 4Cs were in the front of the notebook and there was a website where comments could be left.

The feedback forms and the other ways of collecting comments were refined as time went on and as 4Cs expanded, but Gloria always kept the scheme as simple as possible both for her sake and for the clients' sake.

One of the best ways of getting feedback was the regular meeting – every two months – at The Hub, for clients, families and friends. It was a way of communicating with a good cross section of clients, of giving them the chance of feeling that they weren't on their own but were part of a community, and informing them of and discussing developments in 4Cs and in the local social care scene, which was coming together as an integrated service. (See 'The Careshire Social Care Managers' Network' in Chapter 7.)

As a leader of good care, you will want to know what your clients really think of your care. Is it good enough? Are your clients supported to live their lives as best they can? What could be done differently? Who is the best carer and why? Who is not so good and why? Would it be better if the evening meal was at 6.30p.m. rather than at 5p.m.? A regular questionnaire for clients, carers and relatives can certainly be useful as part of this feedback. It does have the advantage of proving to the regulator and others that you have a questionnaire! Let them think of it as 'quality assurance' if they like. However, there is no substitute for talking and listening both individually and in groups, because this is more likely to lead to genuine participation in running the service. And that brings us to the subject of communication.

COMMUNICATE

Whenever there's more than one person present, communication is going on…even when people are trying not to communicate. Care is communication. Relationship and communication are the same process. As soon as you communicate, you form some sort of relationship. So communication is the essence of the core task of any care service.

Care workers must be good communicators, and that includes being attentive listeners and close observers of non-verbal communication. Social care organisations need a constant flow of communication with all the various means of communication integrated with each other.

Working (as we always do in this book) from the core task, we build a system and practice of communication focused on care. So let us think from the client outwards.

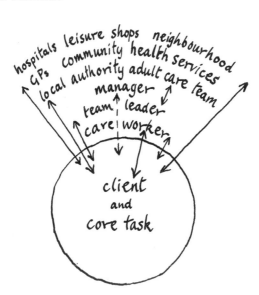

FIGURE 5.2 LINES OF COMMUNICATION TO
AND FROM CLIENT AND CORE TASK

Assuming that an assessement of needs and a plan to meet those needs have been made by the client and one of a number of possible professionals (including a social worker), and that the work has been allocated to one or more care workers (all involving complex and extensive communication), we start with the communication between the client and the care worker.

Client and care worker communication
A CARE WORKER'S CHOICES AND DECISIONS

While the care worker will be following the care plan that the client has been helped to draw up, they must also be responsive to whatever situation they meet. They communicate when they ring the bell or knock on the door...yes, there are many different ways of doing it, and all have meaning. For example, there's insistent ringing and there's coded knocking. The way it's done may announce who it is: we often have a 'signature' ring or knock. Then there's a greeting (good morning, hello, how are you?), and so on. Within the first 30 seconds of contact, much communication has taken place. The worker probably knows how the client is feeling, and the client may know how the worker is feeling.

Crossing the client's boundary (see Chapter 4) – house, flat or room – has already required skilled and sensitive communication. Communication multiplies and deepens the closer the care worker approaches the client and the task. Consider how the worker is dressed. What do they communicate by the clothes that they are wearing? What is communicated by protective clothing, for example, aprons and gloves? If the worker is in the client's house or flat, where do they put their coat? Do they change their shoes? Does a home care worker go straight for the logbook, or get on the phone, or use a hand-held device to record the visit? Or, if the client requires personal care – say, help to get washed and dressed – does the worker communicate that there is sufficient time by the way they behave? Does the worker pick up the clues that this client would like to do things differently today? She doesn't want breakfast and she's worried about her cat, which hasn't come in yet.

The care worker has to listen and be alert to every clue (communication). At the same time they have to make decisions and there are tasks to be completed before they go. Should they go out and look for the cat? Should they at least make sure that the client has got some breakfast? Is the problem really the cat? Check the food in the fridge... Oh, and the medication and there's a prescription to collect... And all this must be recorded in the log book... And, my God, I've only got ten minutes left and I haven't done any of the things on the care plan, and even though the cat's not here, the litter tray must be emptied and cleaned. Will she be OK until the evening visit?

The worker tries not to communicate her anxiety, but she's picked it up from the client as soon as she walked in the door, and she will take it to her next client. But, let us suppose that this care worker is one of your staff, be they a residential or domiciliary worker. They will be working in an organisation that has been designed and is run to support them in the core task. There will be support at hand or at the end of the mobile phone that the worker is carrying. The domiciliary care worker sits down with the client and she phones the 'office' or one of her colleagues. She explains the situation, she gets some advice and support and the schedule is slightly rearranged. The client has listened and added a few comments of her own. Both she and her care worker feel better. The cat hops nonchalantly in through the cat flap. All the essential things get done and the two women laugh together as they part.

What happened? Anxious client – anxious worker – all too much – worker receives support – client receives support – basic tasks get done (principally getting dressed, breakfast and medication) – cat comes home – worker and client relax. In retrospect, the client enjoyed the morning's drama and keeps chuckling about it, and the next day they have time for a cup of coffee together and chuckle all over again. Good communication, good care.

Care worker to team communication

Since we know that the core task is so demanding, care workers need organised support – a support system – that is specifically designed for the job. They need access to support on the job (as in the example above), and to a formal system of support that is planned and regular.

Handovers

In a care home, regular, full-team handover meetings are essential. One 'shift leader' simply going through a list of residents and briefly reporting to the next shift leader is inadequate. The whole team needs to meet for the handover, so that each of them can report their work or hear the reports of those going off duty, reflect together on their work and the state of the home, and plan together. When someone has had an especially taxing shift, or a resident is dying or has died, or any important event that has evoked strong feelings (including pleasure and pride), it is important to talk about it, to share it with the team, to be understood, to pass it on, and for the whole team to learn together. Someone may have found a particularly ingenious way of doing something, or picked up clues to a resident's disturbance, or found caring for a much-loved and dying resident very hard to bear…they need to talk about it before they go off duty, and the next team of staff need to know about it. Through reflective discussion, the team learns to look, think and work *beneath the surface* of what is happening.

The word 'handover' expresses something of the care with which information and the feelings that go with it should be handled and respected. Necessarily brief and disciplined meetings, handovers are the cornerstones of good communication in a care home. They are the foundation of teamwork and have strong developmental, training and supervisory elements. They also encourage and support self-confidence and leadership in all staff. Rather than have the shift leader tell the meeting what a team member has done, she tells them herself and, by doing so, she has to think about the meaning and feeling of what she has done. The manager's job is to get handovers established by being there, leading them to begin with, showing how to structure them and then handing them on. By going to handovers frequently, you will keep them on track and you will stay in touch with the daily details of what's happening to residents, staff and the home as a whole.

In addition to handover meetings, team members have to communicate constantly throughout the day and night. Keeping each other informed, checking if a colleague needs help or how they are, getting advice or reassurance, quick changes of plan…all these need communicating.

In non-residential settings, such as day care and home care, there is a similar but less frequent need for very regular communication, handing over and keeping in touch.

Team meetings

Team or staff meetings should be significant events, even if they are weekly or fortnightly. They should bring the whole team together and regularly reinforce that sense of purpose (core task), ethos and culture that are so vital to a social care organisation. Knowing the importance of these meetings, you, the manager, need to both promote and protect them. It will probably be necessary to insist with your proprietor or employer that team members who are off duty are paid to come to the meeting. Whole staff meetings are the time when big issues and plans are discussed.

Community meetings

Much of social care provision is geared towards groups and communities. Even in home care services, where we might assume that clients are supported in isolation, people form groups and communities. In the effort to provide individual care, we tend to forget that most people live in neighbourhoods of some kind. When amongst a person's problem's is 'social isolation', this is unlikely to be adequately attended to merely by visiting on an individual basis if that does not lead to a reconnection with 'community'. The words 'communication' and 'community' are very nearly the same: bring people together; when they are together they communicate and, as they communicate, community is formed.

A good community home care agency does more than individual work. A group of workers, working as a team, communicating as a team, will link their clients with themselves, with their organisation and with the community around them. They will link them with the team and with other systems of community support. Clients will get a sense of a community around them of which they are a member. Community membership is social support.

Treating a care home as a community is more obviously necessary because there are a number of people living together in one place. Nevertheless, care homes can be very isolating places where all the advantages of community are put to one side in the name of individualism and 'person-centred' care. Communities are stronger for being made up of diverse individuals who each bring something special.

So some form of community (communication) meetings will enhance the work. At one end of the spectrum, a therapeutic community, by definition, must meet as a community. It will be where the big decisions and big issues are debated, where the feelings and events of the community are shared and reflected on. The community meeting is the therapeutic community 'in session' as it were. Outsiders are unlikely to be admitted. Everything is brought there to be expressed, opened up and worked on together. In contrast, a care home for older people may have a community meeting once every couple of months, and it will be a much less intensive gathering. Everyone is invited – residents, families, staff, friends, visitors – but it still has the potential to create a powerful sense of community membership and participation and, as it develops, may lead the care home towards a therapeutic community model. A care home for older people can be run as a therapeutic community just as a mental health home for younger adults can be (see 'Gita designs a staff support structure at The Limes' in Chapter 3).

Written communication

I realise that advising readers to be wary of written communication applies to this book as to every other form of writing. So much that is written down is poorly communicated and misunderstood. Everything that I am attempting to convey now in writing, I have also communicated verbally and, I hope, in action, but I accept that I may have got my wording and tone right for some and wrong for others. As a practised writer, I should be good at it but it's not possible to get it right all the time. As a reader, you can't see me or hear the tone of my voice, and that limits the effectiveness of my words. The same goes for all written communication in the workplace.

As always, you the manager lead the way with writing. Most of your writing will be on the computer. Unfortunately, many managers are not competent keyboard users, which means that it may take twice as long as it should to write an email or report. If managers were still at the same stage with their handwriting, it would be recognised as a significant problem that reduces their efficiency and leaves less time for leading the core task in a practical and personal way. Since most written communication is electronic (computer, tablet or phone based), not being able to use a keyboard efficiently is probably a bigger handicap to effective management than not being able to write by hand. (I should also acknowledge that a lack of keyboard competence can be overcome in other ways as voice activated equipment becomes more available.)

So to begin with, if you can't type, go to a class and learn how to. However, being able to type reasonably quickly should halve your time in the office rather than doubling your output! Learning to type isn't the same as learning to write – and thereby communicate – effectively.

Emailing should be quick and effective. Having largely replaced letters (as sent through the post), emails can be formal, are on the record, and have the advantage of almost immediate delivery and receipt. However, you may sometimes catch yourself emailing someone who is in the same building as you, or even in the same room, instead of speaking with them. Talking is usually the better method of communicating, and it's worth considering what you may be avoiding by emailing instead of talking. Of course, there will be times when you need to put the subject and outcome of the conversation in writing, and then an email (sometimes printed and filed in a hard copy) is useful.

Talking is usually the better method of communication because miscommunication is more likely to be corrected as the conversation goes on, while written communications need great care to get them right first time.

Notices are a source of much misunderstanding. Whenever I visit social care services, I find the notices very revealing. How many notices are really necessary? How many are up to date? How many provide information that is useful or interesting? Generally, the answer to all these questions is very few. Notices often point the reader to the intractable problems in a service: staffing, safety and risk taking, money and pay, poor communication, form filling, and even such mundane issues as washing mugs and 'Now wash your hands'. These problems are intractable because their source has not been understood and worked with (see Chapter 3), and a change of behaviour is rarely achieved by writing a notice about it.

I have seen notices like '20 new sheets are missing from the linen store. Return them or the theft will be reported to the police.' That particular notice was on display in a public area of a care home where residents and visitors could read it. It may as well have read like a notice in a shopping mall: 'Thieves operate in this area.' Similarly, a notice warning staff that their pay will be docked if they are late on duty gives a very poor impression. I am not suggesting that you cover up such failures but that you attend to the causes rather than the symptoms.

Spending time in the office laboriously writing emails, memos and notes that would be better spoken amounts to an avoidance of leadership. However, it is often important to make a written record of discussions and to follow up the communication of information in writing. For example, supervision is talking, listening, thinking and reflecting, but notes to record the session are essential for further reflection and for making progress by picking up where you left off. A record may also be needed for performance and disciplinary purposes.

When writing, always consider who you are writing for and then consider what would be communicated if someone other than the reader you had in mind read it. Electronic communication can, and often does, go astray and, even if you think that you've deleted it, can usually be found by an expert. When writing about clients or colleagues, consider what they would make of it if they were to read it.

In all writing bear in mind Rudyard Kipling's rhyme from 'The Elephant's Child':

> I keep six honest serving-men
> (They taught me all I knew);
> Their names are What and Why and When
> And How and Where and Who.

CREATE AND MANAGE RESOURCES
What are the resources of a social care organisation?

People, buildings and equipment, finance, reputation and goodwill, and organisational culture.

People

I think it's a pity that we now habitually think of people as resources. While the phrase 'human resources' recognises that the principle resource of any social care organisation is people – yes, humans – the word 'resource' can seem to detract from what makes people human: emotions and relationships, thought and consciousness, choice and culture. Regarding a care worker as a 40-hour care delivery resource is like referring to someone who lives in a care home as a 'care bed'.

However, people – the care team – are the most important element of any care service (there is no care without them) and leading them is the most important element of your job as manager. In addition to the paid staff of your team are all the other people who participate in care: partners, family and spouses, friends and relatives, volunteers and visitors and, of course, your clients. As the leader of the service, your job is to focus all this potential on the core task, because it's very common for the 'human resources' of care services to lose focus. It has happened that care homes, in particular, can become the setting for groupings, cliques and rivalries that effectively divert energy, effort and attention from the core task to such an extent that it is forgotten.

Buildings and equipment

While there will be some small home care organisations that are managed from home, most social care services have premises and equipment of some kind. Whether they are rented, leased or owned, it makes sense to look after them. Appearance does matter and a scruffy workplace detracts from the core task, as well as, perhaps, being dangerous and inefficient.

No building is perfect, but some are better than others. You probably make the best of your own accommodation and people have different priorities according to their circumstances. If you've got small children, you are likely to be particularly concerned about safety, so with toddlers in the house you may put a gate across the stairs and childproof catches on cupboards, but there comes a stage when their nuisance outweighs their safety value. As children grow up and if you can afford it, you may consider extending your home so that they can have their own rooms. And when your children leave home, the extension, after being empty for a while, becomes an annexe for an elderly parent. You adapt your home to circumstances; you respond to need. Apply the same thinking to your service's premises.

As the leader of your service, make the best of your premises and adapt them to the job they do for your clients. Buildings and equipment can so easily become obstacles to progress in the minds of the team, and in your own mind: 'Everything would be fine if we had more room' (or a new computer or a new carpet or a bigger garden).

Many small care enterprises started with the proprietors and leaders making do with what they had, and they were all the better for it. And many ready-made, 'state of the art', palatial care homes start with everything in place, and fail badly. Sometimes a team works together in a cramped and inconvenient office where they have to squeeze past each other and share equipment and space, and then they move to spacious, modern, well-equipped offices and they miss the camaraderie and huggermugger of the old place. Installing a drinks machine that dispenses a range of hot drinks in disposable cups may not be the gift to a team that it at first appears to be. What happens to the care for each other that came with making your colleagues a drink, or the conversations while waiting for the kettle to boil, or the team-testing and team-building arguments about the washing up?

How you look after, cope with and use buildings and equipment is very much to do with leadership and a systemic view of social care: being clear about the core task, understanding the feelings that are beneath the surface and in which relationships are rooted, taking the lead and initiative, and deploying and adapting resources to the needs of your clients.

Of course safety, maintenance and regulations matter, and the requirements must be complied with to standards that are probably higher than you would meet in your own home, but these are just resources to do the job; they are not the job itself.

Finance

The money side of care cannot and should not be cut off from the therapeutic body of care. A social care service that is set up with the primary task of making a profit will fail its clients. Equally, a service that is set up with no regard for sensible finance and where money is no object will also eventually fail the clients, although it may be more difficult to understand why.

People needing and using social care are lacking some of the essentials of social, emotional and physical or material support. The job of your service is to provide some or all of these missing elements to support your client.

Clients who are paying for their own care will want value for money, and if they feel that they are being overcharged or exploited, their sense of injustice will undermine their sense of wellbeing. They and their relatives have a right to know how the money that they pay for care is used, and they are more likely to trust a provider who is open about finances. Clients will be more willing to take part in the running of a service they feel is in some way 'theirs'.

In the same way, it is good for staff to know how the money is spent, so that they too can take responsibility for the running of the service and understand how their contribution and their pay is part of the whole. Staff will look out for ways in which resources could be used better and they will have a stake in the success of the service. Team members will feel accountable to each other and to the clients, and they will appreciate the cost of sickness and absence.

The income of the service must match the outgoings. When setting up a service, much more money has to be invested and spent than will initially be earned. A building, equipment and team have to be ready to accept the first clients. For example, a care home will not be full from day one. This investment must be recouped and interest paid on borrowings. These are issues for staff and clients to understand.

There will be repeated fluctuations in income and expenditure as people (staff and clients) come and go. As the service becomes established, the fluctuations should begin to level out. The staff stay longer and an effective team is built; a consistent way of working based on tried and trusted theory and method is established. Getting to this point entails huge investment and commitment not only of money, but of time, energy, ideas, belief and emotion. Proprietors, managers and staff who keep faith with the vision of a therapeutic service and build a team and a way of working will all have invested very heavily. It will have had a profound effect on all their lives.

In a small venture, the effect of just one client being taken on or leaving can make the difference between credit and deficit. While some expenditure can be adjusted to client numbers, staff costs (accounting for well over 50% of outgoings) should not be subject to short-term fluctuations.

Consistency and reliability are essential for your clients, and staff need the same from their employer. If the employer demands short-term fluctuations in expenditure, the staff may respond with short-term fluctuations in their commitment. Very quickly, mistrust and relationship breakdown spread through the organisation, depriving the clients of the essential care and concern that your service is there to provide. In no time, the commissioners (who arguably may have caused the crisis in the first place by underfunding) are withdrawing clients, or clients themselves decide to go elsewhere. Back to square one!

This whole scenario arises from the failure to make money and resources an integral part of the whole ecology of the service, and thereby an essential part of the your responsibilities. The manager – and to some carefully judged extent, the staff and clients – must have responsibility, accountability and control over expenditure, and it must be within the manager's remit to plan spending over whole-year periods.

In order to plan and to make this work (and make the service work), you must have financial information. The information itself is not complicated: whole income, whole expenditure, investment and expected profit margin. You must know exactly what is spent on staff including additional costs such as National Insurance and pensions, and be able to review monthly figures. Similarly for food, cleaning materials, maintenance, recreation, etc. The figures for staffing are readily available because staff are paid every month. Some of the other expenditure may not be accounted for under separate headings, but this can be achieved very easily. If you are not given the full picture – everything – you may suspect (especially at times when spending is being cut back) that the proprietor is manipulating or exaggerating the figures to force urgent action. A feeling of panic and instability spreads.

Balancing income and expenditure over a period of time (not weekly or monthly but annually) is essential to the therapeutic task. Care must be costed and paid for. If a conscientious and honest provider cannot provide good care (and make a modest profit) for the fees, then I would argue that they should not continue the attempt because the care will not be good enough.

The provider (unless directly managing the service) is not in a position to make the daily (or weekly or monthly) judgements and decisions about spending because she or he cannot be sufficiently in touch with the immediate needs of your clients and the service as a whole. But if you don't have the information about income and expenditure which would enable you to make these essential decisions and to plan ahead within the proper limitations of the income, the service and its task will be repeatedly undermined by a 'feast or famine' culture, which is no way to do the work.

LEAD TEAMS AND WORK ACROSS BOUNDARIES

As the leader of your service, you have the difficult job of being at its centre and working at, across and beyond its boundary (see Chapter 4). The conventional manager will work in the office (at the centre) and go to meetings outside (beyond the boundary), but will merely be managing the service, not leading it. Not much leadership takes place in the office or in other organisations' offices, or at conferences, care shows and training events.

Leading from the front means being there, where the work gets done (see 'Identifying and dismantling defences at The Limes' in Chapter 3). We have seen how a social care system can – and does – configure itself to distance and protect the workforce and management from the anxieties provoked by the core task and how, as leader, you have to build a system that contains and works with those anxieties, and thereby enables close, therapeutic relationships to thrive. The 'office work' and the lure of 'office hours' draw the social care manager away from the core task. Managers may complain that they don't have the time to be with staff and clients, but they find it easier not to be. Arriving at the service you manage at 9a.m., going out to a meeting at 10.30, returning at 2p.m. and working in the office until 7p.m. is a long day, but very little of that time has been spent with your team and the clients. Even the supervision session and the team meeting that you had planned have been postponed because someone outside demanded your attendance at the morning meeting, and then you had to spend five hours completing the end-of-month returns for the head office.

If you intend to lead your service to achieve the core task (good care), you have to take control of your time and job, and only then will other people follow your lead and take the same control for themselves. So each week, make time to be with and work with your frontline workers. Depending at what stage your service is, this may be whole shifts or half an hour a day. If you lead a seriously failing care home, work a week with the day care staff, another with the night staff, and then in the kitchen, and the laundry, and with the domestic staff, and so on. Even when you have to work in your office, do an hour with the staff before you start, have breakfast with the residents, sit on the sofa with a resident for 20 minutes watching the news on the telly. You will learn so much and so will the team.

Use these times to understand what the pressures are for the team and how the work goes wrong. Talk, listen, think, imagine, plan and, as you do so, things will start changing just by themselves. But then you follow it up with written feedback – this is what I saw happening, this is how I was feeling, this is how we might change things, this is the plan. Connect it all up...because you are creating and changing a whole system. You actually have to work the night shift and the early shift to understand why residents are being got up too early or being left in bed too late, why the laundry hasn't been done, and why the day staff blame the night staff and the night staff blame the day staff!

And this way you'll be leading leadership. With your example, the staff will lead and begin to take responsibility and make decisions, energy is generated, the whole place begins to fizz with initiative and ideas.

If you lead a home care service, make a point each week of accompanying one of the team as they make an early morning or weekend call. The effect on that care worker will be so supportive and positive; the effect on you will be equally powerful, as will the cumulative effects on the team.

Get organised

To sustain this sort of leadership and to have a wider systemic effect, you will be saying 'no' to your head office and outside organisations. You will prioritise your time to lead your service to carry out the core task. That will mean that supervision, team meetings and being there with your team when the work is being done have a higher priority than most external demands, especially those that arise from poor external organisation. The answer to a call to attend a meeting at the head office on a Tuesday morning may be, 'I'm sorry, but you know I have supervision on Tuesday mornings, followed by a full team meeting after lunch.' Mischievously, you might add, 'I can be with you at 8p.m. on Tuesday evening if that would help.' Similarly, if the regional director turns up unexpectedly on Tuesday morning and wants to meet, she or he will get the same answer. They must organise themselves around you, your service and the core task, not the other way around.

However, if your supervision sessions on Tuesday morning and the team meeting in the afternoon are planned on the basis of 'if we've got the time', and if they rarely start and finish on time anyway, you will not have the resolve to resist your head office's blandishments to join them in their disorganised avoidance of the core task. A social care leader structures the organisation to be reliably supportive with the capability to contain the anxieties inherent in the task.

Social care managers and staff habitually justify their lack of organisation with the explanation that in this work you never know what's going to happen, so planning and organisation are a waste of effort. The very opposite is true. Without a holding structure to contain the reactive anxieties engendered by care, individual therapeutic responses will be closed off and staff cannot work as a coordinated, collaborative team. (See 'Establishing a therapeutic foundation and framework' in Chapter 3.) The same need for organisation applies to you as well. You too need structured time boundaries to work within, not to defend you against or detach you from the anxieties inherent in your job and the core task, but to enable you to work with those anxieties by protecting you from the encroachment of outside demands. (Encroachment in this sense is invading or breaking your time boundaries.)

Rotas

In all social care services, regular patterns of work are vital to the wellbeing of clients and staff. The capacity to adapt to clients' needs depends on having a reliable work schedule. The rota should be designed for the core task but has to take account of staff needs; otherwise you will destroy your principle resource. It may be simpler for most care staff to work 12-hour shifts and have at least three days off each week, making them available for overtime on at least one of those days, but it won't provide better care and it won't be good for staff. It may be simpler to have the same people working together on shifts and have no crossover between day and night staff, but it will result in cliques and rivalries, poor communication and poor care.

Creating a suitable staff rota is particularly complicated in care homes where three shifts a day are required 365 days a year. Most people (and particularly women who make up the majority of the workforce) have other caring roles. People need to be able to plan ahead because each person's absence – for any reason – requires someone else to be at work to fill the gap. Temporary and agency staff can be more of a liability than a help, although having a 'bank' of trusted and experienced part-timers who can be called on is very helpful. Night staff (in care homes) will feel isolated and clients will suffer unless they are fully included in meetings, handovers and supervision, all of which must be planned and rostered. And the integration of housekeeping staff with the whole team is supported by including them on the rota. In any service that operates night and day, 365 days a year, housekeeping staff are needed in the early morning and evening, and at weekends and bank holidays. Being 'on the rota' pulls team members together around the core task.

Don't leave yourself out of the rota. It's good for your team to know what hours you work and when. If you sometimes work at the weekend, early, late or at night, put it on your rota. There will be staff you rarely see who will notice when you plan to be on duty and will want to talk with you. If you do not plan ahead and reserve time for yourself and time with your team and clients, you will soon be working 'office hours' and be at the beck and call of everyone outside your service and very few inside it.

Across boundaries

While as leader of a service, you first attend to the core task and organise a system of care focused on that task, your service is not 'an island, entire unto itself'; it has a context (see Chapter 1) and a boundary (see Chapter 4). The boundary of your service both demarcates it from and connects it with other different organisations and systems, and your own wider organisation or company. Communication and work (transactions) across the boundary are essential and inevitable and, as the leader of your service, you manage this cross-boundary work.

In the earlier example of your head office asking or telling you to attend a meeting or your regional director turning up unexpectedly and assuming that you will meet with her or him, by firmly sticking to your planned priorities you will be marking out and reinforcing boundaries. You have at least two purposes here: first, to maintain the internal organisation (including internal boundaries), and second, to build sustainable and supportive boundaries with your wider organisation. The second clearly requires collaboration across the boundary but in most cases it will be you the manager who leads it. Such is the power of organisations to entrench unconscious defences against anxiety that your regional director or any other headquarters managers will be unlikely to understand the hidden meaning of their attempts to disrupt your leadership and the containing structure you have created. While you may feel angry with them for these repeated acts of apparent sabotage, try to approach them with the same gentle but firm insistence that you would a member of your own staff who was unwittingly up to the same game. Try not to forget that you too play the game (we all do); and that your objective is to work together across boundaries, not to fight a personal battle.

Inevitably, fuelling the anger and creating the sense of a personal battle will be your own projections onto your manager or supervisor resulting from the sometimes unbearable nature of your task, and a supervisor who can both accept and tolerate those projections and help you to take them back will be a superb support for your leadership (see 'Uncontained feelings and the need for containment' in Chapter 3).

Working across the boundary with other organisations

All the stories of managers (Gloria, Gita, Geoff and Gill) in this book are of them taking the lead and working collaboratively across boundaries. They do not wait to be told to do this; collaborative responsiveness is an expectation of their leadership role because good care is achieved only by team and inter-organisational working. People's needs can rarely be compartmentalised and, if services don't work together, clients will lose out.

Where boundaries are clear, respected and used constructively, it is quite possible for allied services in one area to create a comprehensive social care service (see Chapter 6). Where the will and skills exist to do this, and where managers take the lead and the authority to set up their own professional networks (such as action learning sets and managers' coordinating and support groups), the most formidable barriers to change may be the very organisations which should be collaborating, coordinating and regulating care. Statutory commissioners and funders (such as local authorities and the NHS), the senior managers of provider organisations, and the regulators, rather than practising integration of services by facilitating cross-boundary working, may obstruct it and tie it up in red tape. The specialising, standardising, competitive and divisive nature of some of these organisations hampers integration and collaboration across boundaries.

Throughout this book, our managers' stories illustrate how by responding directly to a person in need, creating good care to meet exact needs (the core task), by services dovetailing with each other (because managers are working together across boundaries) and by involving clients in the running and evaluation of their services, the upper levels of social care can become somewhat redundant and intervene to prevent cross-boundary working. The positive response from the most senior levels of management is to redeploy their own resources into support for service managers' cross-boundary collaboration.

Leading successful cross-boundary work requires high levels of confidence, trust and authority. Managers of social care can and do give each other support across the boundaries of their organisations. Some providers encourage their managers to take the lead and find support in this way, and they reap the benefits in reputation, stability and income. Their managers experience the benefits of earning a high status in their professional networks and in the local community, and the satisfaction of being part of a comprehensive and integrated community social care service. Other providers discourage such collaboration because they believe that their business (whether for profit or not for profit) will prosper only through competition, secrecy and the standardisation of their service, and by using rigid management processes. Under such conditions, it is unlikely that a manager will be allowed the authority to make decisions, work across their boundary and thereby to take full leadership of the service they manage.

PROMOTE HEALTH AND WELLBEING

What else would a social care manager do but promote health and wellbeing? Social care is a health and wellbeing service. People come to social care to improve their health and wellbeing and, of course, the 'health' part of this objective is all-round health including mental health.

If, as many social care providers claim, the service is 'holistic' (and so it should be), and we are thinking here about the whole person, then it is the culture and environment of the service that improve and sustain health and wellbeing. This is not confined to care homes: home care services have a culture and environment too.

As manager, you may competently organise and administer all the parts of the service, and for some clients that may be sufficient to maintain their health and wellbeing because they are sustained in other ways by other people or interests. A client paying for a 'care hotel' service would probably prefer a relatively neutral culture and environment that does not impinge on their way of being and living. They get food of a good standard and their medical needs are attended to efficiently; the premises are well maintained and hygienic. They do not want more from the home.

However, most clients want or need much more. Most people want an indivisible combination of care and relationship, the experience of reliable and competent practical help given by a person whom they know and trust, and whom, although paid, they can call a friend. Someone who is thinking about the client as a person whom they respect and even love; who is therefore keen to see that the client takes the right medication at the right time, that they eat and sleep well, that they are clean and feel as good as they can about themselves, body and soul. Someone who thinks about the client when they are not with them, who may send a postcard when they are on holiday, who knows about the client, their family and their life.

Most people who live in a care home want the full package – the home as well as the care. They want a physical environment that expresses love, care and respect, a room to call their own, and a building and garden that feel comfortable, homely and safe.

This sort of social care that clients can feel truly cares for them, with which they can identify and to which they can make a contribution, cannot be achieved simply by competent management; leadership is required.

Take, for example, medication, seen to be one of the most important components of health and wellbeing, and one that provokes much anxiety about risk and compliance.

The administration of medication in a care home and in people's own homes, where care workers often have to manage it, can be seen as a discrete area of the work, deserving its own routines, procedures, rules, risk assessments, training and tests of competence. Medication records are nearly always examined by regulators and a mistake or gap signifies a serious breach of standards. So medication is an area on which a manager must focus in order to demonstrate that the service is safe and effective. This is how we get to the point in some care homes where the most senior member of staff on duty spends two hours in the morning pushing a drugs trolley, giving people their 'meds'. At the same time the home may boast of its 'person-centred, holistic care' and, after examining the records, the regulator (inspector) may conclude that medication management in this home is compliant.

Apart from the inspector, is there anyone who is really happy with this situation? Even the person who is avoiding the bigger responsibility of leading the team (as the senior worker on duty) is possibly dissatisfied with this way of managing medication. (They have to cut corners in order to get through the 'drugs round' by leaving the trolley open sometimes, and initialling several administrations all in one go, and avoiding getting into conversation when a resident asks, 'What's that one for?')

A leader of good care considers this issue from the starting point of the core task rather than simply falling into line with the dictates and requirements of outside bodies, which are concentrating on the isolated issues of medication management and compliance with regulations. The leader manager will engage the residents, staff and possibly relatives in thinking about medication as just another part of good care, as they would in their own homes with themselves or their families.

So what is needed is a reliable and safe way of handling each resident's medication. First, where should it be kept? In an individual medication cabinet in their own room? Can they manage their own medication? If not, who is the best person to help them or to take on the management for them? That would be the person who helps them with all the other complex, personal and vital support that they need. There is nothing particularly different or special about medication that marks it off from the other demanding care tasks; indeed, it is often a lot more straightforward than some (for example, helping someone to shower and get dressed).

A leader of good care creates a shared culture in which staff are united in their commitment to the core task and dedicated to the best, safe, loving care – the health and wellbeing – of each resident. They are trusted and respected. They have training in each aspect of their work, so they can manage medication just as well as they can use a hoist or listen to a client's worries, as well as they can cut toenails or sit with and care for someone who is dying, or speak with relatives, or write the notes at the end of their shift. They have regular individual supervision and report to the handover meeting at the end of their shift. So why separate the administration of medication from all the other essential tasks of caring?

PROTECT PEOPLE (STAFF AND CLIENTS)
FROM EXPLOITATION AND ABUSE

The obverse side of care is neglect and abuse (see Chapter 3). Whenever exploitation and abuse hit the headlines, there are desperate efforts from government downwards to 'ensure this will not happen again', usually leading to new rules and instructions, and a great deal of 'putting procedures in place'. It is also likely to involve more attempts to standardise care, thereby reducing the close personal relationships that are at the heart of real care and increasing management activity to prove that the rules have been followed. The new procedures are a reaction to a gross failure in a particular care service, but are then applied to all other services irrespective of their record or their ability to prevent exploitation and abuse. While it is compulsory to follow the new rules, as a leader you will know that the only difference they are likely to make is to divert more of your precious time recording that you have followed them.

Knowing that care created through relationships involves bad feelings as well as good, you will encourage the surfacing of those bad feelings in appropriate settings such as individual supervision and team support sessions. You help your team to understand and acknowledge that bad feelings exist alongside good, caring feelings (that they are systemic), that you have bad feelings too, and that everyone in this work needs to be able to talk about them rather than act them out (see 'Establishing a therapeutic foundation and framework' in Chapter 3 and a letter to *Caring Times* in 'Denial' on page 77).

Furthermore, such bad feelings are attached not only directly to caring, they will come from conditions of employment, from the organisation and from past experience – in the family, at home, in relationships, at work, at school, as an infant or child. So 'putting procedures in place' may feel like some sort of reprimand or punishment, and exacerbate the feelings and make it even more likely that they will find expression and release during contact with clients.

As a leader, to some extent you have to protect staff and clients from the very rules that have been imposed ostensibly to 'safeguard' them. Yet you will find within the framework of 'safeguarding' processes that will be helpful if used in conjunction with your systemic approach to protection, which will work at the root causes of abuse and neglect. So, as with some other externally imposed rules and procedures (see Chapter 6), turn what may at first seem to be a predominantly irrelevant and bureaucratic framework into a positive process that can be used to the advantage of clients and staff. (You will find the advice in *The Social Care Manager's Handbook* very helpful.)

The mistreatment of clients is almost always associated with the exploitation, neglect, bullying and mistreatment of staff. As well as giving them the opportunity to talk about their bad feelings towards clients and themselves, think about and listen to them about their feelings towards you and your employer. It is hard for anyone to remain committed to caring for people if they are not cared for themselves. An employer who pays as little as possible and thinks so poorly of staff that their support, training and development are neglected is running a business that has the mistreatment of its clients built in. A home care worker, dashing from client to client, physically unable to complete the minimum of care tasks but at risk of losing her job if the care record does not concur with the care plan is going to skimp on the care and falsify records. Some employers prefer care staff who are vulnerable on the grounds of poverty, family responsibilities, immigration or minority status, and the threat of unemployment because they are unlikely to complain. As a leader of good care, you must protect your staff and be prepared to fight a poor employer on their behalf and, if necessary, do what you would expect your staff to do if they saw mistreatment: blow the whistle on your employer.

WORKING WITH EXTERNAL AUDIT AND INSPECTION

As with 'safeguarding', external audit and inspection did not come about because most social care was good but because there have been many exceptionally poor examples of care. And again, as with safeguarding, as leader you must find a way of putting an imposed and compulsory process to productive use. Regulation and inspection have themselves been through various waves of failure, revision and reform, and have been at times been described by politicians as 'unfit for purpose'. When they themselves have been subjected to external audit, regulators have been found wanting. Nevertheless, regulation of social care has the force of law and must be accepted.

The term 'registered manager' refers to the person who has been judged by the regulator as suitable by experience and qualification to do the difficult job you are doing and who is thereby made accountable for the service. Currently the questions that an inspector will consider when making an assessment of your service are:

- Is it safe?

- Is it effective?

- Is it caring?

- Is it responsive to people's needs?

- And is it well led?

The exact wording of these questions applies to the English regulator, but all regulators should ask broadly the same questions.

These seem relevant and sensible areas to assess, although inevitably they overlap. You could regard the questions as looking at your service from different angles, all pointing to the central question of 'Is it caring?' A truly caring service (after all, care is the core task) is safe, effective and responsive to people's needs, and if it is all of those it is sure to be well led. It is significant that the word 'led' is used rather than 'Is it well managed?'

As with several other external institutions overlooking your service, the regulator remains conflicted about what its job really is, how it relates to the core task of your service and how you should relate to it. Questions that continue to be asked are: Should the regulator deal with complaints? Is it an improvement agency? Should it give advice? Is it consistent in its judgements? Is it expert enough? Should it award 'quality ratings'? Who is its client? All these questions have had different answers over the years and are likely to go on being debated, making inspectors themselves inclined to be dogmatic in their insecurity and to inspect on the basis of an earlier set of standards and operating principles.

As the leader of your service, you need an inspector who will understand how your service works and give you useful feedback. If you can see their job from their angle and have a respectful expectation that with your help they can do it well, you are likely to get the best out of them. Of course, the same goes for your own staff and most outsiders (see 'Inspection at The Limes' below).

Keep your inspector in touch with what's going on in your service, not only through the communications and notifications that you are obliged to make, but tell them of any events, changes and plans that are significant. Encourage and cultivate them: not in the sense of flattering, bribing or buttering them up, but in the expectation that as a fellow professional, they will be interested in and welcome the information you give them. And if they don't seem interested, just continue as if they did.

While your proprietor, chief executive or regional manager may want you to manage your service to 'pass' inspections, and therefore to prepare and present all the records and information with the objective of making the inspector's work as easy as possible, as leader you know that is not your job. The inspector should see your service as it really is, so all the paperwork and records that they wish to examine or sample should be what is produced and used for the core task. You should have to do no additional work solely for the purpose of inspection. You work for your clients and the core task, not for the regulator.

No service is perfect and nor is any manager. Like other regulators who visit your service, your inspector is more likely to do a good job and to provide useful feedback if they feel they are being treated with respect as a fellow professional. Neither aggression nor subservience will get the best out of them.

INSPECTION AT THE LIMES

Within two months of starting as manager at The Limes, Gita was faced with an inspection. She had been chosen and appointed by Sarah, the company's managing director, to lead radical changes not only at The Limes but with the intention of initiating a transformation in the way the whole company ran their care homes. She had discussed the implications of this bold plan with Sarah and they both knew that to be effective such a change would take time and would encounter many obstacles. While they had both anticipated some of the difficulties and resistance ahead from inside and outside the home, in the company and from the regulator, the reality of the resistance – and failure to comprehend the process of change – was more entrenched and pervasive than they had expected.

Gita's predecessor as manager had been highly competent in the skills of compliance, which is why she had been moved to one of the company's persistently non-compliant homes, but it was also one reason why real change at The Limes was so difficult. This inspection had been triggered by the arrival of a new manager (Gita), and by several complaints to the regulator resulting from the changes that Gita was already leading by her radical actions of working alongside the staff and finding out what was really going on (see 'Identifying and dismantling defences at The Limes' in Chapter 3). The complaints had come from dissatisfied staff, residents, relatives and even from social workers.

For two years before the previous manager left, The Limes was a fully compliant service. The home had appeared to be functioning well but, beneath the surface, there were all sorts of deals, deceptions and compromises that had to be undone. Deep down, staff and outside managers felt guilty, and a further layer of self-justification had been spread over this guilt by the 'fully compliant' accolade of the inspectors.

After all, they were only doing what everyone had to do: if you wanted your service to prosper, you had to produce the goods for the inspector and be judged fully compliant.

What Gita was doing by witnessing and exposing the deceptions was deeply shaming for all those who had connived in the dishonest facade. While it was a huge relief to the majority of staff who were angry and resentful at being compelled to tolerate mediocre and sometimes poor care, those who had accommodated their practice and their consciences to a compliant form of institutionalisation were fearful of being exposed. It's in the nature of such reform that those who reveal the truth are often seen to be the cause of the failures. So in this case, Gita's management was blamed for the failures in care she was exposing by those who had maintained those failures and hidden them beneath a covering of compliance.

The situation was made worse by the regulator's reintroduction of 'quality ratings'. They were now looking to rate homes as 'inadequate', 'requires improvement', 'good' or 'outstanding'. Anything less than good would create major problems for the home in terms of attracting residents and continuing in business. This was not only an additional problem for the providers; it was an extra anxiety for the regulators themselves because there would inevitably be services that they judged to be good or outstanding that were later exposed as neglectful or abusive in some way. The inspectors would have to look a bit deeper than compliance and try to identify the longer-term and more fundamental signs of what they called 'quality'.

Fortunately for Gita, the inspector allocated to The Limes wasn't the person who had previously found it to be fully compliant. She was a very experienced inspector who had survived all the changes in regulation, had found the previous inspection regime to be prescriptive and superficial, and was pleased to have the opportunity to get back to what she would refer to as 'real inspection'.

She arrived unannounced at 7.30a.m. and found Gita with the staff team at their morning handover. From the handover, she learned so much of what was going on in the home. She noted the names of staff and residents with whom she intended to speak later. She had a very quick word with the whole team, telling them what she would be looking for during the day.

Gita took her round, talking about what was happening, what needed to be changed, how she was going about change and about her whole philosophy of care. The inspector was impressed, and so pleased to be treated by Gita as a fellow professional with the assumption that she was well motivated and would be able to understand the complexities of the home.

The inspector stayed until well after 6p.m. She ate with the residents and went to the afternoon handover, where she gave some feedback. Before she left she met with Gita again and told her what would be in the report.

Overall, the rating at this stage had to be 'requires improvement', which, after all, was why Gita was there and why she was making changes. Was it safe? There were certain practices that were unsafe but they were already noted and work was being done to make them safer. Was it effective? Not very, because there were many institutional and defensive patterns of work that undermined the core task. Was it caring? There was a lot that was caring, and quite a lot that was routine and detached. Was it responsive to people's needs? Yes, but there were instances – noticed throughout the day – when residents clearly needed help and got little or no response. And was it well led? Yes, exceptionally well led.

Gita could not have been more pleased with the feedback. Her decision to trust the inspector and talk candidly with her was vindicated. She had been at The Limes only seven intense weeks, and to have this external, knowledgeable evaluation and feedback about the home was just what she needed. It could have been the opposite with an inexperienced and 'compliant' inspector, too timid to make a judgement for themselves and too worried about ticking all the boxes for their manager. The effect on staff was galvanising: they were going in the right direction and, contrary to expectation, the inspector appreciated what they were doing, gave no succour to the nay-sayers, and the 'requires improvement' rating gave them hope and something to aim for.

The draft inspection report, when it arrived a few days later, was very disappointing. It did not capture the tone of the inspector's verbal feedback. The understanding, appreciation and encouragement had been stripped out, leaving a stark and rather damning account of all the things that were wrong and 'required improvement' and few of the things that were right and had already been improved. There was no discussion of context and nothing about what lay beneath the surface or what work was being done at that level. No one who didn't know the home could have read the report and failed to conclude that this was not a good home to live in, to work in or to visit.

Gita phoned the inspector to protest. The inspector said that she couldn't discuss it on the phone and asked if she could meet Gita to talk. They met the next day. The inspector explained that in order to be consistent and fair to all providers, the regulator's policy was to exclude from reports all the background context and organisational analysis that would describe and explain what was going on in a service. The report was designed to give a neutral assessment and to describe exactly what the inspector found on the day of the inspection. She said that she had hoped with the new inspection regime it would be possible to give a more rounded and informative picture of the home, but her manager had cut large chunks out of her report wherever she had tried to elaborate on the background and the process of change that she had seen in action at The Limes. The regulator could not risk being wrong. What if these changes at the home were to come to nothing and there was some public scandal? The regulator would again be exposed to public criticism for supporting a process of change that seemed to result in neglect or abuse.

While she was sympathetic to the inspector, Gita felt let down and angry. She was angry with the regulator, which had promised reform and yet had reverted to its previous defensive position, more concerned about its own survival than getting on with its important job. It was modelling a form of command and control, compliance driven management that had played a leading role in determining the uncaring culture at The Limes that she was now changing. And she felt let down by the inspector who, she had thought, was going to be an ally for this change and who, as a knowledgeable outside professional, had offered such useful feedback and could offer more in the future. For a few days Gita had hoped that the regulator would help her; now she had to accept that was not the case. She resolved not to let her disappointment and anger alienate her from the inspector. She still needed the inspector to be interested, involved and supportive of the changes taking place at The Limes. She would stay in touch...and be friendly.

LEAD PROFESSIONAL DEVELOPMENT, INCLUDING YOUR OWN

This book is part of a movement for the professional development of social care managers. A wide range of people (including thousands of 'registered managers') and organisations are the instigators and supporters of this movement (see the National Skills Academy for Social Care Registered Managers' Programme in 'Books and Other Resources'). We believe that improvement in social care will be led by you, the managers, not by any of the outside bodies, or at government level, although they all have the responsibility to enable, resource and support you to take the lead.

The best learning and professional development in social care occurs on the job, in supervision, handovers, team meetings and training sessions, reflecting on work, writing about it, thinking and talking about it... learning, learning, learning every day. As manager, you lead a learning culture: you not only learn but you teach every day, and the culture grows. There is a vast range of learning materials, including books, videos and online resources that can be used for training (see 'Books and Other Resources').

STAFF DEVELOPMENT AT 4CS

When Gloria went to assess Mrs Smith's care needs (see 'Accepting a new client at 4Cs' in Chapter 4) and Mrs Smith asked her if she would be her care worker (because they got on so well), it made her think about the separation of assessment and care. It would be much better if her colleagues could do their own assessments, although the tradition in home care always had been for an 'organiser' to assess and then a home care worker to provide the support. Gloria began to make all assessment visits with the colleague who was likely to become the home care worker for the client. To begin with Gloria took the lead, and then, as colleagues learned how to do the assessment, they took over. Each of the local teams had a lead assessor who then taught their colleagues in the team until everybody was qualified by appraised practice to make a care assessment.

Everyone who works in your service should feel that it is a place of learning and development. Everyone becomes a learner and a teacher (including clients who have much to teach…and learn).

This internal culture of learning and development, like the core task itself, needs external supplies: qualifying and specialist courses, seminars, lectures and action learning sets, visits to other services, conferences, and so on. Expect everyone to attend outside learning events and then to bring the ideas and information back to the team in the workplace. You take the lead and set the example by reserving time for your own learning and development and by contributing to outside events so that the team feels that their leader and their service is part of a larger progressive movement for change.

THE LEARNING CULTURE AT THE WILLOWS

The Willows is a small therapeutic community for people with learning disabilities. Gill, the manager, is aware of the danger of such an apparently specialised social care service becoming isolated and introspective. In practice, The Willows is very much a part of its local community and strongly connected with wider professional practice. Gill encourages staff and residents to take ideas, skills and information from the home to the social and professional community around them, and always to bring new learning back and share it in the home.

Training and professional development are on the agenda of every team meeting, and every member of staff is expected to contribute. Those on training courses report what they have been learning. If someone attends a conference or seminar, they are expected to bring something of interest and relevance back with them. If someone has read an article, seen a television programme or listened to a radio programme that has made an impression, they are asked to talk about it. The team learn to present ideas and information, and involve their colleagues, so leading a discussion is encouraged.

Gill sets the tone by doing what she wants her team to do: she is a leading member of the Careshire Social Care Managers' Network (see Chapter 7), she has a mentor, she regularly attends professional meetings and seminars, she writes articles for professional journals and she supervises the senior team members and, initially, all new staff. She expects everyone in the team to be learning and contributing to each other's learning, and she sees every opportunity for learning and development as a contribution to the learning culture of the home. For example, Gill encourages staff and residents to get involved with sports training, art and craft classes, history and philosophy, gardening and do-it-yourself, cookery and flower-arranging. Often staff and residents are learning alongside each other and then, together, bring back some new interest or activity to the home.

CONTENTS OF THE CHAPTER FOR DISCUSSION

This chapter challenges much established thinking and practice. Each section provides a subject for debate and could be used in team meetings, training sessions and action learning sets:

- Lead with values and principles: Believe in what you are doing. *Is your heart in your work?*

- Leading the core task. *In the face of many distractions, how do you keep on task?*

- Involve and support clients in running and evaluating the service:

    ○ Clients running and evaluating their own services.

    ○ 'Quality assurance.'

    ○ *In what ways do you or could you involve the participation of clients?*

- Communicate:

    ○ Client and care worker communication.

    ○ Handovers.

    ○ Team meetings.

    ○ Community meetings.

    ○ Written communication.

    ○ *Discuss the strengths and weaknesses of communication in your service.*

- Create and manage resources:

    ○ What are the resources of a social care organisation?

    ○ People.

- Buildings and equipment.

- Finance.

- *How creative and imaginative a social care artist are you with your raw materials?*

- Lead teams and work across boundaries:

  - Get organised.

  - Rotas.

  - Across boundaries.

  - Working across boundaries with other organisations.

  - *Think about your service's potential for collaborative work and how it will benefit clients.*

- Promote health and wellbeing. *Which is more important for a client's health and wellbeing – truly close, caring relationships or compliance with procedures and regulations?*

- Protect people (staff and clients) from exploitation and abuse. *Explore and discuss the causes of exploitation and abuse.*

- Working with external audit and inspection. *How might you build a good working relationship with your inspector?*

- Lead professional development, including your own. *What are you doing to develop as a professional and a leader?*

Discussion of the stories

- 'Mrs Smith and The Hub Club': Is there a role for day centres and 'clubs' and, if so, what are the arguments for and against?

- '4Cs feedback from clients': Does 'quality assurance' have a valid role to play in social care, or is it just a regulatory requirement? If it does have a valid role, how should it be used? How do you 'assure quality' in your service? Client and care worker communication: Apply the points from this example to your own service. How do your staff negotiate their way across their clients' boundaries? Clothes, uniforms, protective equipment? Recording? Who's in charge, client or worker? Decisions about timing?

- 'Gita designs a staff support structure at The Limes': Discuss ideas and your own approach to staff communication – handovers, team meetings, community meetings, written communication.

- 'Inspection at The Limes': What is your experience of inspection? Which aspects of Gita's experience and feelings do you recognise? How might you or do you manage inspection so that it benefits your clients?

- 'The learning culture at The Willows': Discuss the building blocks of your service's learning culture.

6

CHANGING PLACES
TURNING BARRIERS TO LEADERSHIP INTO ENABLERS AND SUPPORTERS OF LEADERSHIP

While your service is dominated by the demands of outside bodies (such as regulators, commissioners, central and local government bureaucracies, and even by your own employer organisation), it is very difficult to step up to your leadership role and keep the core task at the centre of your service. While you have a responsibility to lead, all these outside bodies have made commitments to enable you to take on your role in full, and that means that they have to change their relationship with you and your service. If social care is to change for the better, they have to change and, like most of us, they are used to pointing to the need for change in others without understanding that change involves them. They have to move off your ground and be clear and active in their own roles of supporting the core task that you lead and manage. So their awareness and understanding of the core task, boundaries and roles, and an acceptance of their responsibilities are essential in supporting you as the leader of your service. Whole-system improvement in social care depends on your determination as leader and their willingness to allow you to lead.

TURN IT THE RIGHT WAY UP AND IT WILL WORK

Consider for a moment a simple wooden chair. A chair is for sitting on. It may be used for other things but if you turn it upside down, it's of very little use at all. It would be nearly impossible for anyone to sit on a chair when it's the wrong way up. If you tried, you would find that the legs and cross rails got in the way, and might even injure you. The legs of a chair are essential for supporting it and the weight of the person sitting on it, but if the chair is turned upside down the legs and the whole chair cease to be functional.

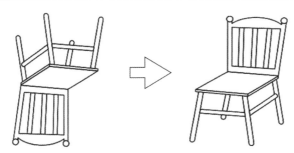

FIGURE 6.1 TURN THE CHAIR THE RIGHT WAY UP AND IT WILL WORK

Once all those outside organisations that dominate social care understand what the core task of your service is, and what their role is in supporting the core task, you will be enabled to lead the service with their help. Like the legs of an upside-down chair, your own external management, the regulators, local authorities and national government, and commissioners may feel important and powerful in a position above you, and may believe that your function is to be subservient to them. But the reality (obvious to the public) is that in this position, they are worse than useless; they can damage your service and prevent you from leading it. In turning social care the right way up, we will transform the role of outside organisations and they will become the enablers and supporters of your leadership.

FAILURE DEMAND: THE NOOSE THAT STRANGLES INITIATIVE AND LEADERSHIP

If your whole working life is taken up with trying to prevent organisational failure, repairing damage and dealing with the resulting complaints – in other words, with 'failure demand' (see Chapter 2 and John Seddon in 'Books and Other Resources') – you cannot lead because you're not going anywhere. Failure demand is an endemic disease that can infest any organisation. It is the demand that is created by repeatedly doing the wrong thing and then dealing with the results of failure. Large organisations pass the infestation on to smaller organisations, until a whole system – such as social care – is infested.

> Big fleas have little fleas upon their backs to bite 'em.
> Little fleas have lesser fleas, and so ad infinitum.
> And the great fleas themselves in turn
> Have greater fleas to go on.
> While these again have greater still, and so on.
>
> *The Siphonaptera* (Augustus De Morgan, based on
> Jonathan Swift's 'On Poetry: a Rhapsody')

This systemic infestation starts at and is spread from the top. Government, on a five-year electoral cycle, has only a short time to take the initiative and to make long-term structural changes. From then on ministers concentrate on damage limitation, window dressing and bribery in the attempt to persuade the electorate that they are worth re-electing. It's like buying a dilapidated house: if you don't attend to the crumbling foundations before you renew the roof, repair the fabric and decorate, you will be for ever after patching up, papering over the cracks and tarting it up to sell it on before the structural (or systemic) faults make it uninhabitable. After the first few years in office, governments get blamed for whatever is going wrong, and they spend the rest of their term reacting to the failures that are caused by long-standing fundamental faults. By reacting to failure and by attempting to prevent further failure (trying to 'ensure this will never happen again') they tighten the noose, regulate and standardise, and strangle variety, initiative and leadership. Similarly, local authorities, hospitals and care providers react to failure by 'putting systems in place' to deal with failure until much of their activity is concentrated on reactive procedures, reviewing mistakes, instituting new complaints systems and auditing processes, all in the name of quality assurance and performance management.

It is as if, from government level downwards, organisations are confronted by double incontinence. Rather than finding out why and how to tackle the causes, they rush to 'pad it up' – to wipe away all traces of shit and to slap on a thick, absorbent pad, thereby ensuring that incontinence is permanent. Part of the process of perpetuating failure is to elevate the recording and auditing of useless work to the high status of a statutorily required task by which the 'quality' of a service is measured.

Shock-horror headlines trigger macho reflex reactions – just fix it! – and new rules and procedures are instituted to hide or correct failure, leading to another round of failure. What is not understood is that the failures are merely symptoms of underlying faults: the symptoms can be hidden (by papering over the cracks) for a while, but this cannot lead the system to real change and development. In papering over the cracks, you build in further failure down the line, which only adds to your problems in the long run. Whenever we see individual problems in social care being singled out as if they can be cured by issuing pronouncements from ministers, followed by new procedures, rules, record keeping and audit, we see failure demand in operation.

A lack of dignity in care is a symptom, and no matter how much money a government throws at it, and how many 'dignity champions' are trained and appointed, the causes are left untouched. Of course, new work is created for consultants and training companies, and a whole new mini dignity bureaucracy is established, but dignity is a result of empathy, respect and self-respect in caring relationships and cannot be commanded by a dignity policy. Nor can any of the other single-issue outcomes that government attempts to fix so that they can demonstrate to the electorate that they have 'got a grip' and are taking action.

To challenge these almost universally accepted and seemingly benign initiatives is to question the motivation and good sense of the whole social care establishment. This is much easier and less risky for an author than for a social care manager who might put their job at risk by doing so.

With failure demand being the default mode of social care, how can a registered manager resist being overwhelmed and surrendering? The pressures to collude, conform and comply are great. You may struggle to find any support at any level for your attempt to reverse the trend and to lead from the front (see Chapter 7).

Without the constant challenge of the core task and asking: 'Is what I'm doing now necessary to carry out the core task?' all systems of care settle into the default mode of failure demand, which is an institutional defence against the anxiety engendered by the task (see Chapter 3). To return briefly to my analogy of the upside-down chair: it is as if the legs of the chair cannot bear to perform their proper function. It is much easier not to bear the weight of the chair and its occupant but rather to stick up in the air in a posture of self-importance, while the blame for being useless is attached to the seat of the chair on which it is impossible to sit. The chair works only when the legs support the seat.

THE PROBLEMS THAT TRIGGER FAILURE DEMAND

What are the common problems for a social care manager that create this cycle of failure demand? Regulatory non-compliance; contract monitoring by local authorities; safeguarding; absenteeism, staff sickness and staff shortages; incomplete or out-of-date records; medication; moving and handling; inadequate training and supervision; low pay; staff attitudes; falls; complaints. Dozens of things can and do go wrong and, as a manager, you rush around trying to fix them. Equally there will be dozens of eager consultants and companies ready and willing to paper over the cracks, to make you compliant with the standards, to lift that embargo on placements from the local authority, to write new policies and procedures and to fill those vacancies.

To sum up: too much management time and energy is spent dealing with failure, or what's gone wrong, instead of getting it right in the first place. Health and social care policy is 'driven' (from the rear) by defensive reactions to what's gone wrong, and managers feel they have no choice but to comply. Driving change is the opposite of leading change. It is impossible to drive deep change, yet the word is used repeatedly in the same way that 'deliver' is used in conjunction with care. This is the 'white van' (see Appendix 1), driving and delivering model of care and has little in common with the growth of reciprocal human relationships, the loving kindness and empathy that are at the heart of care.

To end this cycle of failure takes determined collaboration at all levels. First, we have to acknowledge and recognise that the cycle exists and that we all play a part in it, and then we have to take stock of the situation and lead our service by restoring the core task to its proper position (see Chapter 2). However, managers will struggle to do this on their own. It would be like trying to sit on that upside-down chair and at the same time attempting to turn it the right way up.

TURNING A CARE SERVICE THE RIGHT WAY UP AT 4CS

Gloria turned home care the right way up by joining with colleagues to set up 4Cs (City and County Care Cooperative). After spending years working for two unsatisfactory organisations, first the local authority and then a private home care agency, she used all she had learned as a home care worker and manager and, with half a dozen friends and former workmates, she became a social entrepreneur.

It took the original team a year from their first evening meeting to set up the cooperative. They had to work at it in their spare time – meeting, planning, drawing up their business plan in order to borrow the money to get started. They had to invest money of their own and work all hours in their existing jobs to earn a living for themselves and their dependants.

They learned so much from doing it all themselves, and they were energised by the experience. Gloria had analysed the problems of the way home care was currently run from the top down, with the owners creaming off a large profit and Careshire (the local authority) paying as little as it possibly could. Caught in the middle of this were the care workers and their clients, cheated out of a living wage, decent care, dignity and respect. In addition to diverting resources into undeserved profits, the companies were wasting resources by their highly centralised bureaucratic approach. They employed three tiers of manager – local, regional and national; they had head office and regional HR and 'quality' directors, and a central media and public relations office, as well as a large finance section. Such a complex and hands-off way of managing the organisation matched Careshire's approach to commissioning home care from 'independent' providers and was reminiscent of the way in which they had run their own in-house service when they had brought in a new manager to 'modernise' it.

When Gloria first worked for Careshire as a 'home help' in the 1990s, the employment conditions were relatively good because there was a strong union to protect the workforce. However, the union itself was distant and hierarchical, so the workers were even then caught between competing bureaucracies, neither of which appeared to understand that the whole point (the core task) of a home care service was to meet the needs of the clients. Nevertheless, Gloria and her colleagues were able to organise their own work while the council and the union busied themselves with matters that had little to do with providing care.

In those days, Gloria worked with a group of six other home helps on one of the council estates where there was a large number of specially built flats and bungalows for elderly and disabled people. They knew all the clients and all the clients knew them.

The team met once a week with their organiser (manager) in the home help office, but the real organisation (management) took place directly between the team members. All their clients had diaries or a care log, and the home helps kept their own diaries. They started each week with a rota and this was adapted as the week progressed. Their clients had phones (landlines in those days) and the team kept in touch with each other throughout their shifts. If someone was going to the chemist or supermarket, they collected prescriptions or groceries for more than one client. If someone got held up, they would alert a colleague nearby to call in at their next scheduled visit. If one of them had to attend a school meeting or doctor's appointment, that could be accommodated. Holidays were worked out between them, cover arranged amongst the team, and the organiser was informed. This collaborative and flexible way of working was so successful because they were all committed, as a team, to the core task. For them, their clients came first and they never let them down. They had created their own unofficial organisation within the local authority. Working this way was very satisfying and rewarding. They were all known on the estate and valued for their work.

Gloria worked with this team for her first four years in the UK. Although the wages were low, the conditions were relatively good and, in spite of having two university degrees, Gloria found the work stimulating and engaging, and she felt that she was making an important contribution to her community.

Unfortunately, there came a time when all local authority services had to be put out to competitive tender. Management consultants were brought in to evaluate all directly employed council services, and when they came across the work of this collaborative, responsive and extremely efficient team of home helps, they didn't understand what they were looking at. A new home care manager was recruited to 'modernise' the service and prepare it for competitive tendering. The teams were broken up and reorganised centrally and the service all but collapsed. Within a year, most of the staff who had been employed by Careshire were re-employed by private companies that had successfully tendered for the work, one of which was headed by the manager who had modernised the old home help service.

Gloria didn't give up, although she was very unhappy about the loss of the old team. She continued to work with the new company and was soon promoted to a management post. Within the severe constraints of a hostile work culture, Gloria worked hard and did her best. She won the respect of the huge team that she was given to manage and the trust of the many clients whom she had to assess before allocating support workers. She took the opportunity to learn the business from top to bottom. She was regarded as a great asset to the company and was in line for further promotion. People trusted her. However, Gloria was not intending to stay because she was out of sympathy with the company's policies and the business model. The owners were interested only in increasing profits at the expense of both workers and clients, and she felt that the better she managed, the higher the profits would be, and that was the only reason she was valued. So she led a group of her old colleagues, some of whom still worked with her, to set up 4Cs and provide care in the way that they had done when they worked as a team for the council, but this time they would be in control.

It took several months to get established (see 'Accepting a new client at 4Cs' in Chapter 4), but by a total commitment to the core task 4Cs soon became the 'go to' home care provider in Careshire.

HOW GITA TOOK CHARGE OF THE LIMES

The Limes is owned and run by a large international care provider. It was opened with some fanfare four years before Gita was recruited to become general manager. Along with 20 other new care homes owned by this company in the UK, The Limes has a standard design – always referred to as 'state of the art' – with large en-suite bedrooms, a cinema and hairdressing salon, a bar and a 1950s styled and furnished 'reminiscence' room. By the time Gita was recruited to the general manager's post, the home had settled into a mediocre existence, compliant with all the regulations and of little trouble to anyone including the owners, regulators and local authority. While at the top of the company some managers recognised that The Limes had stagnated and that, if it ever had been 'state of the art', it had long ceased to be so, it was always fully occupied and continued to earn a profit for the shareholders. The previous manager was asked to move to another home that inspectors had found 'non-compliant' and which needed her 'steady hand on the tiller' to bring it back onto the course of compliance, full occupancy and, therefore, high profitability. The company offered substantial bonuses to managers who kept their homes full.

Gita was different. While she recognised that any care home had to pay its way, that those run by profit-making companies had to do more than pay their way and that care homes had to be 'compliant', none of these was a reason for the care home's existence. The core task was good care for the residents and that might take time to achieve. She would spend at least six months restructuring and reorganising the home and its care practice, and changing the whole ethos. During that time it would probably not be full and it may not be compliant. Indeed, Gita knew that this sort of deep change would create discord and uncertainty, resulting in an impression for many that the home was going downhill and that Gita didn't know what she was doing.

Gita had applied for the job and been appointed because it had been advertised in a way that invited applicants who could lead major change. The company had a new managing director Sarah who, after rising through the ranks, had at last got into the position to lead the changes she herself had envisaged but failed to achieve as a care home manager. Sarah knew that compliance and full occupancy were not enough. She wanted the company's homes to be different from the boring and second-rate mainstream. And she wanted them to have a character of their own and to be rooted in their communities rather than being an over-branded branch of the company. These were risky ambitions, and she would have to be shrewd and determined and very persuasive if she was going to achieve them. Sarah had already lined up some allies in the company, and she herself had been appointed as managing director because the chair of the board shared her desire for leading the company in a new direction. Sarah knew that to achieve this change she would have to appoint care home managers who could lead the changes on the ground. Gita was her first such appointment.

There were many problems at The Limes. The previous manager had gathered a little clique of staff around her. They were mostly senior staff but they included the administrator and a couple of the nurses who were sometimes meant to be in charge of shifts. The home worked on the basis of treats and rewards: meals out together, prizes and vouchers to favoured staff. This was consistent with the culture of the company. The full occupancy/profit margin bonus payments went to the manager, her deputy and the in-house salesperson who 'sold beds' at the home on commission. They, in turn, passed on some of the rewards to those below them. The general manager had a good deal of discretion when it came to staff recruitment, selection and promotion, but major aspects of running the home were determined at head office level. When Gita was first appointed, the housekeeping, catering, menus and provisions were all managed from the head office. The menus were the same in all the homes in the company. The furniture and decoration were all supplied by the same firm and were renewed regularly. All staff wore company uniform, company name badges and answered the phone with a standard company greeting. Even staff meetings, supervision and training were standardised. The quality assurance and complaints systems were the same in every home. Gita's predecessor was happy to leave all these decisions to the company (they made her job easier) but Gita was not.

If Gita hadn't picked up from the advertisement that the job involved leading major change, and if she hadn't – both at the interview and subsequently – been given a clear message that she was expected to lead a shake-up in care practice and in the management and administration, she would not have taken the job. However, she also realised that she would meet resistance to change in the company, the local authority and the regulator, as well as in the home.

When Gita first proposed changes to the catering – cooking, suppliers and dining – she was met with blank incredulity from head office, followed by a lecture from the finance and contracts director, and a visit from the Director of Quality Care. (See a later part of this story in Chapter 2, 'The core task is the whole task'.) They all treated her with barely disguised contempt and reminded her that, as the general manager of The Limes, she was still on probation and was jeopardising her post by questioning long-established, evidence-based company policy. Gita took care to copy all her letters to Sarah, the managing director (MD). This further annoyed the head office staff, who had detected the rumblings of change at the top but could not believe that Gita would be allowed to get away with such revolutionary behaviour.

With remarkable courage, Gita phoned Sarah and asked for a meeting. While she was willing to fight her own battles, she felt that it was high time that she got support from those who had knowingly put her in the position to lead change on the ground. Sarah was evidently struggling with the headquarters staff and managers, but Gita insisted that she was given the backing to forge ahead on all fronts with changing The Limes. She would set out a programme of change, send it to the MD and expect Sarah's open, clear endorsement to go ahead. She rightly argued that she had enough to do leading the changes at The Limes without doing the MD's work as well. The ground must be cleared at the head office for these changes to have a chance of success.

Gita's plan was radical. She would start with food and catering, meals and mealtimes, but before any planned change could take place she had to take stock. She did this by working on shifts with every member of staff – nurses and care staff (days, nights and weekends), kitchen, housekeeping and maintenance staff. Senior staff in the home were angry with her for not spending enough time with them, and those who had been part of the previous manager's clique obstructed the changes that Gita was leading and gossiped to resentful contacts in the company's head office.

For the first year of change, almost everything seemed to get worse. There were many complaints. Within two months of Gita's arrival, an inspection found The Limes to be non-compliant in several ways, demanded an 'action plan' and said there would be another inspection within six months to check the plan had been carried out and the home was compliant. The complaints and the inspection created massive 'failure demand', making it extremely difficult for Gita to concentrate her time, energy and effort on getting things right rather than investigating, reviewing and reacting to what other people thought had gone wrong or to the mischievous allegations intended to undermine the changes. There was huge pressure on Gita and on Sarah at the company level to revert to proven – or, as they liked to claim, 'evidence-based' – practice. Those who had been resisting the changes redoubled their efforts, and the morale of those who had been working alongside Gita sunk.

Gita found her strength to persevere from the other managers in the Careshire Social Care Managers' Network, through their action learning sets, through her mentor and through her friendship with Gloria, Gill and Geoff, who supported her personally and professionally throughout. Sarah needed as much support as Gita did but she didn't have the same resources. However, Sarah did remain strong in the face of hard opposition within the company and amongst board members, and this enabled Gita to win through after two years of struggle. (See 'How Gita took charge of The Limes' in Chapter 7 for the next part of the story.)

HOW GILL HELD ON TO THERAPEUTIC COMMUNITY PRINCIPLES AT THE WILLOWS

The leadership and management of a therapeutic community may at first sound contradictory. To many observers a residential therapeutic community is synonymous with a 'commune', and such a community cannot be led, let alone managed. However, the way The Willows was designed, run and led was intended to enable the residents to lead their own lives through the good experience (including the difficulties) of living together in a *therapeutic*, learning and mutually supportive community or household. The group is as important as the individual.

Such a community has to be designed and led with discipline and purpose because, while the principles are based in ordinary, everyday ways of behaving and relating, they don't fit easily into a society (context) where care is ordered and 'delivered' in 'packages' and plans. The care that is found in a therapeutic community comes almost exclusively from human relationships and relatedness, from finding a way of living together as a community.

When Gill decided that Martha had to leave The Willows (see 'Gill asks a client to leave The Willows' in Chapter 4), she had few clear allies. She made the decision by thinking of the core task of the community, and the need to hold it together and protect it so that it could get on with the task. People within the community, half the staff and most of the residents (apart from Edwin and two others at the time) were sympathetic, although few staff would have made as difficult a judgement for themselves. Gill had the toughest challenges from her own management in collusion with social services, which paid for Martha's place. The inspector, who was involved by Martha's social worker, was also unsupportive.

People and incidents like this (Martha and the behaviour that led to her leaving) not only define and refine the core task, but they can also lead to clarifying the boundary, roles and principles of an organisation. Due to Gill's resolve and discipline, this instance led to reviewing and renewing The Willows' therapeutic principles (see 'Formative clients: The clients that help to shape and clarify the core task' in Chapter 2).

Reacting to pressure from social services and the threat of losing placements, Gill's regional manager passed on the pressure to Gill to keep Martha. She increased this pressure when she was contacted by the inspector who called into question Martha's human rights, her safety and the safety and freedom of choice of all the residents. In an effort to appease the commissioners and regulators, the regional manager was in danger of undermining the therapeutic foundations on which The Willows was run. Those calling for Gill to allow Martha to stay had little experience or understanding of therapeutic community work and, while strong on policies and procedures, could therefore not link the principles to the practice.

Gill took her difficult, pressurised situation to her action learning set, where she found the process of telling her story and receiving candid, insightful feedback extremely helpful. From that meeting and from a discussion with her mentor, she was able to go back to her regional manager, who was also her supervisor, and persuade her to support the principles of therapeutic community at The Willows (see Chapter 7).

HOW GEOFF'S LEADERSHIP IS THREATENED AND RESTORED BY GROUP ACTION

As the director of The Hub, Geoff leads a loose and changing conglomeration of people and organisations that use the resource centre. While social and community care groups are the main users, there are other groups whose overt purpose (or core task) is not care but whose activities are beneficial to some users of social care services. There is a management board for The Hub. The board is elected at the Annual General Meeting and the director is appointed by the board and reports to them. Geoff's role is complex and there are times when dealing with the board is the most difficult and frustrating part of the job.

The Hub is housed in a former Careshire care home that was closed. The whole building is now managed on a long lease by a local housing association. The upper floor has been converted into one-bedroomed extra-care flats with two of them reserved for short-term rehabilitation. 4Cs provides the care to the flats. Most of the ground floor is used regularly, every day and most evenings, by a wide variety of groups, most prominent amongst which are 'clubs' (all referred to as 'Hub clubs') for young and old and middle-aged people with all sorts of special needs and interests in common. There are lunch clubs, tea dances, book clubs, memory clubs, domino and bingo clubs, gardening and music clubs, and outside there is a basketball and five-a-side football pitch. There are also various clinics and surgeries, a laundry and assisted bathing and showering facilities. People can drop in to The Hub without having some event, club or clinic to attend. There's a cafe and information desk, and people use The Hub as a meeting place. The Careshire Social Care Managers' Network meets there.

Each user group has to manage their own work, meetings or event but Geoff has to manage the whole place so that all these groups work together for the greater good. He has to be firm but flexible, sensitive and resilient. He's dealing with professionals who are rivalrous and pushy, and with volunteers, some of whom are dependent on him for support and encouragement. On top of it all, he's dealing with a management committee who are by turns self-important, interfering, demanding, unreliable and unreasonable, and sometimes supportive and enthusiastic. Much depends on who is chair of the management board.

Geoff is the first director of The Hub. He was appointed by a sub-committee and reported directly to the chair of the board. This worked very well to begin with because the chair had been a leading light in setting up The Hub and she retained the enthusiasm, principles and idealism of a founder member. She was a wheelchair user who had battled most of her life with unresponsive and inadequate services. She had an independent overall view, passionate and determined about community development and support, but truly impartial and incorruptible. She saw the same in Geoff: they had an excellent working relationship. However, Geoff felt that it would be sensible to tighten up many of the informal arrangements that worked so well but could lead to problems down the line.

Quite unexpectedly at the AGM, the management board elected a new chair. The new chair was also chair of the housing association that leased and managed the whole building. She owed her election to the knowledge, competence and drive she demonstrated as a board member, impressing her colleagues and making them feel safe because she seemed to know the ropes of the money and regulations.

This new chair started from the position that The Hub was not making sufficient money to be 'sustainable'. Charges would go up, contracts would be renegotiated, free groups would be ended; after all, who was paying the bills? She questioned the need to employ staff directly for cleaning and maintenance because it would be cheaper and more efficient to have this done by a private contractor as the housing association did on its own housing schemes. (One of these directly employed staff was Edwin, who was in charge of the grounds.) She wanted to set up user satisfaction surveys and quality monitoring of all user groups and organisations. She had asked them all to produce a 'social impact assessment'. She represented the board members who also came from the larger and more bureaucratic organisations that had an interest in The Hub as users and/or commissioners, including the Careshire Council representative, and all of whom found the previous regime disturbingly loose, informal and risky.

After three months of the new chair's 'reign', The Hub was transformed. Under the threat of redundancy, some of the staff (including Edwin) became demoralised and either went off sick or came to work but refused to take responsibility. Many of the smaller groups had left already, unable or unwilling to comply with the demands of the board of managers. Several of the regular clubs which obtained some funding from the local authority to support elderly and disabled people continued but in a more formal and less congenially self-governing way, and the volunteers for these groups were draining away. The lunch club had lost its conviviality and attendance had dropped significantly. Most of the tenants of the extra-care flats used to come to the lunch club because they met friends and there was always so much going on in the place, but now they preferred to stay in their flats and have a home care worker prepare them a snack lunch that they ate on their own. And, of course, the income of the Hub plummeted, which was taken as proof that more cuts were necessary.

Geoff looked for another job, but doubted that he would find one that had the excitement and satisfaction that he'd experienced during his first couple of years in this one. He knew that moves were afoot to attempt a revolt but he had to be careful not to be identified as an instigator. There were many groups and individuals who had also experienced the power and liberation that The Hub had engendered. People had felt that they could change things for themselves by banding together and joining up with other groups. They had not been totally constrained by the lack of resources (mainly money) or by the strangulation of rules and red tape that they had previously experienced in social care organisations. And this had been in no small way due to the way that Geoff had managed The Hub on behalf of a board (and chair) who understood that The Hub's purpose (core task) was to provide, enable, and support *them* to take control of their lives. Because of this experience, a 'Save The Hub' group was formed, determined to fight for what they were losing. They used the local press, radio and television...and social networking. They pressured local councillors into speaking up for them. A group stood at the gates every day with a banner, talking with passers-by and with everyone going in and out. The staff called in their union and pressured them to take up the cause.

Edwin, who lived at The Willows, went off sick when at first he heard about the changes that the new chair was proposing. His job would go and he felt he would lose everything: his status, his pay, his identity. He felt important at The Hub and he loved his job. He managed the grounds, the car parking, the deliveries...everyone who came to The Hub knew Edwin. He was appreciated and valued. Geoff depended on him. And, not least, Jean, his new girl friend, was a helper at the Hub clubs, and they saw each other nearly every day. Jean was also in The Hub Caps (volunteer group) and was trying to get him to join, but now he felt all that would go. Edwin talked about losing his job with his friends at The Willows, most of whom were also users of The Hub. They were annoyed with him for going off sick. It was like the time when Martha had latched onto him and he'd just gone along with it; and then, when Martha had been asked to leave, he'd spent all day in his room moping and not talking to anyone. His friends said they'd come down with him to The Hub. He should go back to work and fight this. There were several discussions in community meetings, and Edwin went back to work and his friends from The Willows joined the protests in opposition to the plans.

The 'Save The Hub' movement gathered strength. Those groups and individuals who had felt they had to leave were contacted and returned. The people from the extra-care flats came back to the lunch club and the Hub clubs started up again. There was a 'Save The Hub' committee meeting every morning to organise the day.

Geoff and other Hub staff had to steer a difficult course between just carrying on with their work and being directly involved with the 'Save The Hub' committee. They were still legally employed and contracted to the board of management, but by keeping the daily running, maintenance and administration of The Hub going, they were assisting the 'occupation' and the protest. In the face of the threat to the whole ethos and future of The Hub, the place was now flourishing, but Geoff was worried that it couldn't last because they didn't have legal status or control of the finances. However, there was widespread public support and the local media were now firmly behind the occupation (it made great pictures and reports), so the chair and committee had to decide whether to attempt to take back control or to surrender it.

The chair resigned and the previous chair was re-elected, and gradually 'order' was restored. As director, Geoff had the tricky task of rebuilding the organisation after its liberating and somewhat anarchic experience. In addition, trust had to be rebuilt at all levels between the leaders of 'Save The Hub', him and the management board. It took a further six months for The Hub to achieve the state of organisation and stability that it had before. At times, Geoff had to be firm with some of those who had so successfully led the occupation movement and who six months later would be panicking when a similar threat arose again. (See 'Containing panic at The Hub' in Chapter 3.)

CONVERTING THE BARRIERS TO YOUR LEADERSHIP INTO SUPPORTERS

You cannot lead good care if people and organisations which are external to your service are in the way, blocking and diverting your work on the core task (see Figure 5.1 on page 120; compare Figure 6.2 with Figure 2.2 on page 46).

FIGURE 6.2 CONVERTING BARRIERS TO SUPPORTERS

Whatever the source of the blockage and diversion (your employer, company, management committee, senior management, regulator and commissioners are all prime candidates for this role), the barriers they put in your way have to be removed, sidestepped or turned into supportive resources.

You are unlikely to be able to do this on your own. In our examples (stories) throughout the book, our four managers find ways of leading their different services so that the barriers are removed and converted into supports for change and development. However, they have to build alliances and partnerships with one or more external people who have influence in and with the organisations or groups that are standing in the way of progress.

Gloria (4Cs) removes the barriers: she accumulates information, practice and contacts from previous employers; joins with a group of colleagues to form a cooperative; builds a home care service that is the best in the area; and gets into a position whereby she can provide a service directly to clients, tailored precisely to their needs and be paid either by them or the commissioners; and lead the service as she, her colleagues and clients think best. The external people and organisations, such as the regulator and commissioners, are then able to carry out their proper functions by checking that the care is good enough for the clients, and checking that they are getting value for money and are meeting the needs of their clients by commissioning 4Cs. Gloria and her colleagues have built a very positive relationship with commissioners by focusing totally on the core task.

Although **Gita** (The Limes) was selected to lead her service and was given the authority to do so by her managing director, she is working for a company that has a top-down, interventionist management culture and a stronger commitment to its shareholders than to its clients. While this is what Gita was specifically employed to change, she encounters barrier after barrier from inside the company and from the regulator. She has only the backing of the managing director to clear the obstacles within the company, and the managing director herself is struggling. Gita has to force the issue, confront the head office opposition, demand more support from the managing director, and build a bedrock of support for change amongst her staff and clients. The next stage of converting the barriers into supports is told in Chapter 7 where Gita finds that the head office staff are beginning to understand what she is trying to do, and that forming a respectful working relationship with the inspector results in a change in attitude from the regulator.

Gill (The Willows) leads a therapeutic community in a voluntary organisation that is committed to this way of working but, because outside managers don't fully understand the principles and practice of a therapeutic community, her manager quickly reverts to conventional top-down management when under pressure. Likewise, both commissioners and regulators attempt to undermine Gill's leadership and block her decisions. In this case, it is Gill's firm grip of therapeutic principles and the strong bonds of The Willows with the wider community, her capacity to contain her own emotions along with the anxieties of the community, and her understanding of the psychological process that impel her manager, the commissioners and the regulator to hide their fears beneath compliance, that enables her leadership of the community to survive.

Geoff (The Hub) has a major obstacle in the person of a new chair of the management board attempting to change the whole ethos of the service he (Geoff) leads. A voluntary organisation (The Hub) is at the mercy of its trustees or management committee who should be running the organisation on behalf of the clients and, in the case of The Hub, the local community. The new chair, along with other committee members, is intent on financial efficiency and tighter control of The Hub's activities to conform with the model of management of her housing association and many other 'successful' third sector service providers. Geoff's first thoughts are to leave but he realises he would be unlikely to find another organisation where his talent for enabling and leading community development could be so valued. He avoids direct and open opposition to the new chair's plans. She has the power to dismiss him, but she does not have the power to compel the community that has built and uses The Hub to comply with her instructions. He does have strong allies in the previous chair and in The Hub's community. The fact that the community, after a faltering start, organises itself to oppose and defeat the chair's proposals, and to take back control of their resource, owes much to the facilitating and enabling leadership that Geoff has provided.

THE CARESHIRE SOCIAL CARE MANAGERS' NETWORK

Had it not been for our four managers' membership of a professional support and development network, it is unlikely that they would have survived in their jobs, turned barriers into supports and led their services with such success. The learning, mutual support and sense of professional comradeship sustained and inspired them.

When Gita was appointed to the manager's post at The Limes, she knew that she would need independent outside support. During her previous job as head of another care home, she had taken a part-time Master's degree called 'Consulting and leading in organisations: psychodynamic and systemic approaches'. The company that she worked for then was willing to give her time and some financial backing to go on the course, but it was unwilling then to allow Gita to use what she had learned. So when she saw the advertisement for The Limes, instigated by Sarah (MD), looking for someone to lead 'systemic change', she jumped at it. It was her understanding and analysis of how social care services work and don't work that qualified Gita for the job and gave her the courage and resolution to take it on.

At about the same time that Gita started at The Limes, Gloria received an email from the National Skills Academy for Social Care offering a grant for social care managers to set up local professional networks of 'registered managers' (those who were registered with the regulator). Gloria was the registered manager of 4Cs (home care cooperative), and although she received excellent support from her colleagues in the cooperative, she felt she needed an external reference group and the stimulation and learning of a group of peers in other social care organisations. So, Gloria contacted three of the people she knew might be interested in forming a network (Gita, Gill and Geoff) and she put in an application for funding an initial round of ten meetings (see 'The Careshire Social Care Managers' Network (continued)' in Chapter 7).

THINKING ABOUT THIS CHAPTER

- Can you identify ways in which the organisation and management of the service that you lead is 'upside down', ways in which you and your service are supporting the external organisations and management rather than they enabling, resourcing and supporting you and your service?

- Similarly, what are the problems that trigger 'failure demand' in your service? In other words, what are you doing (and being told to do) that need not be done at all if the right thing was done in the first place?

- Think about how you spend your time and which activities are most effective in terms of the core task?

- Consider the four stories of changing places:

  ○ 'Turning a care service the right way up at 4Cs'

  ○ 'How Gita took charge of The Limes'

  ○ 'How Gill held on to therapeutic community principles at The Willows'

  ○ 'How Geoff's leadership is threatened and restored by group action'.

Four different managers leading four different services with different pressures – all find ways of changing their service and of achieving external system changes that then allowed their service to reduce failure demand and attend to the core task. Without the support, learning and solidarity of their social care managers' network, our four managers would not have been able to make the wider system changes that they did. If you don't have a network already, take the lead and set one up.

7

STEPPING UP TO LEADERSHIP
AND LEADING YOUR SOCIAL CARE SERVICE WITH COURAGE, VISION AND INTEGRITY

This book has been written as part of a movement for change and development in social care. Social care services can and should be better than they are. Efforts by government and by the upper echelons of the social care establishment make little difference to what happens on the ground because until they accept that they have to examine and reform their own part in perpetuating a failing system and shift their position (see Chapter 6), they are unlikely to be successful in persuading and supporting other people to change. Simply doing more of what hasn't worked is futile.

STEPPING UP FROM A LOW POSITION

Most social care managers feel isolated and insufficiently supported (survey by The National Skills Academy for Social Care, July 2012). They identify the barriers to managing a good service as lack of time and money, too much bureaucracy and too many conflicting priorities, followed by the burden of regulation, fear of making mistakes and contradictory advice. This suggests that the majority of managers are overworked and under-resourced, are overwhelmed by paperwork and don't have a clear core task, are frightened of breaking the rules and getting things wrong, and are told to do things in one way and then in another.

The training that has been available to qualify as a manager perpetuates the dominant thinking of chopping an immensely complex and demanding job into bite-sized chunks which are then fed to managers and ticked off long, repetitive lists of discrete tasks, competencies and standards. The agency responsible for designing the training shows scant awareness that it plays a leading role in the failures of the wider social care system and that if social care is to change it must be part of the change. According to the current managers' training course, the barriers to change are exclusively centred on the service that they manage, whereas we have found that the blockages are whole-system barriers, which are not amenable to isolated management interventions. Amongst the qualifying actions for leading change are: 'identify internal and external barriers that may hinder the service provision fulfilling its vision and achieving positive outcomes for individuals' and 'take action to address barriers that hinder the achievement of the service provision and positive outcomes for individuals'. In plain English: spot whatever is stopping your clients getting good care and remove it. Easier said than done when the barriers that managers have identified are too little time and money, excess paperwork, the absence of a core task, fear of making mistakes and being given contradictory advice.

Managers are trained to follow orders, not to question them, to comply rather than to take the initiative. It is not surprising that many lack the authority to lead. Considering their responsibilities to clients and the large teams they manage, they have a low status both in social care and in the wider society. Working relationships with commissioners, health and social services, and regulators are grudging and unequal. The services they manage are often in competition with other services, and the companies that own and run them (and the not-for-profit proprietors and providers) may discourage too much familiarity with other managers for fear that they might lose their competitive edge. They may also have an unconscious fear of rebellion. Generally, when managers are brought together, it is to be informed of and instructed in some new regulation or procedure. Indeed, so subservient have many managers become that, given the choice of a stimulating and innovative seminar on some new ideas about care, and a session from the regulator telling them what records they must now keep to pass the next inspection (which is all on the regulator's website anyway), they will queue to take instructions from the regulator but leave the seminar room half-empty.

Yet I have written in this book of four managers who are not like this at all. They are not subservient; they have authority and have earned respect; they are not people who can be pushed around. They love their work and they have great ambitions, not just for themselves and their service but for social care in their locality and nationally. They are real professionals with their own high standards; they support and stand up for each other. There are hundreds – perhaps thousands – of such managers, and it is they (you?) who will lead social care to a better future.

So do as they do: take up your role assertively, leading the whole task: at the centre, on the boundary, in the community, with your team, collaborating and integrating with partner organisations and teams. Never forget or ignore what is going on beneath the surface. The losses, anxieties, feelings, needs and unconscious defences against the anxiety engendered by the task are embedded in the system. They are connected with and influence everything that happens in every part of the system. Attempts to rid the system of them will fail and will only add another layer of defence. If your service does not work at that deep level with the core task, it can never be good.

CONNECTING HEAD OFFICE WITH THE CORE TASK (GITA AND THE LIMES)

During the first year of change at The Limes, Gita had been preoccupied with and almost totally focused on creating the foundations and framework for good care within the home. Of course, she had struggled to obtain the resourcing that she needed from her head office, having only Sarah (the managing director) and one or two other allies outside the home.

She had a full-time administrator who, herself, had to be persuaded to back the changes Gita was making rather than continue with the way of working that Gita's predecessor had favoured. (She and the previous manager had spent happy hours in the office together and frequently went out to lunch with other favoured staff.) However, with persistence, involvement, respect and kindness, Gita had gradually got the administrator to adopt a very different way of working, becoming much more involved in the core task, and seeing herself as a vital member of the whole team without whom the resources and necessary bureaucracy for good care would dry up. (For example, processing fees and paying bills efficiently are essential.)

As some of the barriers to effective administration and resourcing within the home were removed, so it became more obvious that similar barriers existed outside in the head office. And, as the home's administrator became more identified and integrated with the core task, so she found that her previously smooth dealings with head office met with obstruction. Gita was able to see this in systemic terms. It was as if the home's administrator had been one of the head office's team but with her office in the home, and now she'd joined the opposing team. In addition, the head office staff were being managed by people who themselves were hostile to the changes that were taking root at The Limes. Gita reasoned that if she could demonstrate to the head office team how important and worthwhile the core task was and what a significant contribution they could make to it they, like the home's administrator, may become backers rather than barriers.

Having discussed and planned it with the administrator, and talked with Sarah about it, Gita invited head office staff, two at a time, to come to spend the day with them at The Limes. They loved it. They met residents and staff; they experienced for themselves the professional work of handovers and mealtimes, and the everyday life of the place. Their fear of the work and their habit of demeaning both staff and residents gave way to interest, involvement and admiration. Now they could see the sense of what they were doing and how it related to good care, and they became keen to remove or reduce some of the unnecessary obstacles that stood between the head office and the home and its work. They enquired after particular residents and chatted to staff they knew by name during phone calls. Gita made sure that these visits became more frequent and always invited head office staff to events at the home. The head office now had a real connection with the core task and could take pride and satisfaction in supporting it.

One of the staff from HR was visiting on a morning when Martha was leading one of her singing groups and, being a keen singer herself, she joined in. She then got her own singing group involved, and the two groups began putting on concerts at The Limes and The Hub, and Martha was welcomed – and much valued for her voice – in a new group.

DARING TO TELL THE TRUTH AND TO TAKE THE INITIATIVE

You and your team are led by the task that is before you. Good care is a response to need. If you take your cue from your clients and their needs, the service system required becomes self-evident: it is designed and built from the core task as the work is done, as the variety of changing needs is met. You create an organisation that works for the primary task. A leader of good care gains great satisfaction from seeing clients getting what they need. Such work is enjoyable and creative.

The emperor's new clothes

Two weavers promise the emperor a new suit of clothes that is invisible to those who are incompetent or too stupid for their positions. When the emperor parades before his subjects in his new clothes, they dare not say anything for fear of losing their positions, but a child cries out the truth: 'He's wearing nothing at all!'

Institutional self-delusion and the fear of engaging directly (through relationships) with the task have perpetuated a highly sophisticated and specialised, over-planned, over-managed and over-regulated, and very expensive, social care system that is so unsuited to its purpose that its resources are consumed by 'failure demand' resulting in the 'delivery' of remarkably little care. The constraints of this system starve those who work in it of satisfaction and enjoyment. When you are the registered manager and your livelihood and future appear to depend on your collusion and compliance, saying that the emperor has no clothes is difficult. When you speak the truth, you may be branded as stupid or incompetent. You know he has no clothes but, with everyone around you appearing to be convinced, as is the emperor himself, that his new clothes are even better than his previous outfit, how do you dare to tell him that he's naked?

While following is the companion of leading, complying is the antithesis. Most of those around you are far from convinced that the current 'care delivery' and compliance system is meeting people's social care needs. The emperor's lack of clothes is obvious to all, even the emperor knows he has no clothes but denies the knowledge. If you are going to lead good care, compliance and collusion will be your enemies and the enemies of your clients. A leader of good care has the vision (to see clearly), the courage (to speak the truth) and integrity (to stand up for what is right), and the resilience (to keep going, through thick and thin). You will find that your colleagues will join you, and at other times you will be a 'leading follower', in other words, someone who has the courage, vision, integrity and resilience to follow someone else's lead.

COURAGE

Taking the lead takes courage. Stepping out in front and saying that you are taking a different route, when everyone else is hurrying down the prescribed route, takes a certain blend of courage:

- the courage not to follow the crowd, knowing it is heading in the wrong direction, and at the same time to be unsure of the way ahead yet to make the best judgement you can and then to act

- the courage to look beneath the surface, to explore the source of unconscious defences and motivations

- the courage to stay with being uncertain, to tolerate confusion and complexity, to allow a course of action to emerge, not pretending to yourself or others that you know what the answers are when you don't

- the courage to put your trust in other people, not to lump people together or split them into good and bad, us and them, and not to turn on them if and when they get it wrong: the courage to take back your projections

- the courage to contain and use your emotions, to think and act with feelings, without letting them rule you

- the courage to examine and question yourself: your motivation, your values, your power and authority, and still use your authority to lead

- the courage to be creative and break new ground.

Courage is not needed when you do as you are told, when you follow the prescribed route, but when outcomes are uncertain, making decisions takes courage because you will sometimes get them wrong.

VISION

'Vision' is an over-used, and thereby devalued, word. At its plainest, vision means sight; at its most extravagant it means a mystical experience as in seeing a vision. In the context of leading good care, it means the capacity to see ahead and to envision where you are going. Systemic leadership requires an awareness of your current position and its relatedness and connection with all that is around (context), clarity about the job you are doing (core task) and the grounded imagination to look ahead and beyond next week to what could be in a year's or five years' time. Vision is the response to the question, 'Where are we going?' Why would your team commit themselves to following or joining you in this adventure if they didn't know where you – and now they – are intending to go… together?

Because of the collaborative, open-ended, emotional and imaginative nature of social care – people creating responsive caring together – it is wide open for leaders with vision and enterprise. Faced with the prospect of leading a care service, the creative possibilities open up before you (the art of managing social care). Share the vision and keep refreshing and renewing it. Don't allow your vision to be blocked, blinkered or obscured by naysayers with their bundles of policies and procedures tied up with red tape. If you lose vision, you will lose the imagination to lead.

INTEGRITY AND AUTHENTICITY

Integrity means honesty, soundness and wholeness. A leader with integrity sticks to their principles, is reliable and resilient, and is a *whole* person, someone who is true to themselves. Authenticity is closely related. Whoever meets you or works with you as a leader will ask themselves, 'Is this person for real?' 'Do they believe in what they are saying and can we rely on them to do what they say they'll do?' 'Are they true to themselves?' Much good work can be done by people who have genuine disagreements as long as each feels the other to be sincere and trustworthy. Differences amongst good trusting colleagues are potentially very productive, and encourage other people to be authentic and open with each other.

RESILIENCE

The core task is emotionally challenging. As leader of that task, the emotional demands are magnified and focused on you. You have to deal with the pressure coming from the task and the management of the service, and from external sources that make insistent demands on you that are often irrelevant to the task. Your emotional survival and health are threatened by the nature of the task and your leadership role, and to continue to lead through all the vicissitudes of your job, you have to draw on your own personal and professional resilience, and replenish and reinforce that inner strength from outside resources such as your peer group, supervision and consultancy.

Leading good care is hard work, mentally, emotionally and physically. There will be times when you are exhausted by the incessant demands, the stress and the long hours. You need to look after yourself and accept support from others. Remember that you are not indestructible.

Resilience stems from the capacity to bend rather than break, in other words to remain flexible and adaptable. This does not imply the surrendering of a principled position; indeed, your ability to hold on to your principles is increased by your agility and manoeuvrability, and your awareness of your own vulnerability.

ORGANISATION

It would be wrong to suppose that these essential aspects of your character (courage, vision, integrity and resilience) will get the job done if we exclude organisation – the ability and will to manage or to organise. If we think of leadership as an expedition: you may possess all these seemingly heroic leadership qualities but if you don't organise the personnel, supplies and logistics, you are unlikely to reach your destination.

Good organisation is the backbone of good care. A disdain for organisation will demean those whose job it is to manage efficiently and effectively. In this book, I may at times seem to have undervalued the management and administration side of leadership, but that would be a grave mistake. What I have criticised is unnecessary, irrelevant and diversionary bureaucracy and rule-making, command-and-control management and distortion of the core task by external bodies.

Effective organisation in your service enables all the real work to be done. In most care organisations excellent administration – rotas, payroll, planning and timekeeping, maintenance, record keeping, communication, supplies, contracts, and so on – must be valued and led no less attentively than the relationships and care, because without administration your service breaks down. These tasks and roles must be integrated into the core task so that administrators know that they are contributing to care and everyone experiences them as helpful, supportive members of the team. The more these roles are brought within your service the better. Like every other aspect of management, the more administration is drawn away from the core task and beyond the boundary of the service, the more it will assume a superior and disconnected position, and the less efficient and responsive it will be in supporting good care.

LEADING FOLLOWERS

If you take the lead, you will need followers because you have nothing and no one to lead without them. Your colleagues and teams need similar courage to follow because the first few people (colleagues) who step behind you and join you will be subject to the same pressures to get back in line as you are. Even when you clearly take the lead, you will always be following because none of us is the first to take the lead in any sphere of life. There were always predecessors, the people from whom we learned, the ideas that led to the way we now think, the enterprise or care system that stimulated our current thinking and initiatives.

So followers are leaders too – whether we are following a leader now and become a leader in the movement that we have followed, or whether we have been handed the baton of leadership transferred to us in the process of reading, listening, talking, thinking about ideas, theories and experience from earlier leaders.

ORGANISING YOUR OWN SUPERVISION

Your manager may not be suitably experienced, skilled or knowledgeable to supervise you. Nevertheless, you have a line management relationship that needs to be as productive as possible. Ticking off lists of jobs to be done, hurried discussions of what has gone wrong and tricky decisions to be made, and anxious anticipation of the next inspection do not amount to professional supervision.

If you are leading good care, you need time with a supervisor who can give their full attention to you, so that for an hour or more you can talk about, reflect on, work on your job, how you are experiencing it, what you are feeling, understanding, learning and thinking. You need a supervisor who has the capacity to listen and contain; to encourage, challenge, stimulate and occasionally confront; sometimes to inform; to take a long view and make connections; and to provide a conceptual framework within which to reflect, think, imagine and plan.

It may be that you can negotiate this as part of your appointment but, more likely, you may have to survive without this sort of professional supervision until you are in a strong enough bargaining position to demand it. Meanwhile, you might encourage your line manager to reserve time for reflection in your meetings.

OTHER FORMS OF PROFESSIONAL SUPPORT AND DEVELOPMENT

As with supervision, you may have to find or create your own sources of other professional support and development. There are always opportunities to learn by attending courses, conferences and seminars, but you will need more than the standard offering. As a leader of good care, you are creating a new and different service, and the support and development needed is different from what is provided for services as they are now. You may consider independent mentoring and coaching for yourself, and consultation for you and your service. An independent consultant can be engaged to help you and your team to work together and explore the issues, especially the unconscious defences of the team and the service. All of this will encourage and aid learning and development.

In addition, you can pursue your own professional interests through various networks and associations, through your reading (books, journals and articles) and perhaps through teaching, lecturing and writing. Don't underestimate your ability to contribute to other people's learning by sharing your experience, ideas and practice. By doing so, you will test, refine and increase your own knowledge.

JOINING TOGETHER IN PROFESSIONAL GROUPS FOR CHANGE

As a social care manager, you could take all this advice, exhortation and encouragement and you could become a near perfect example of a manager! But you would still struggle to survive because the reactive resistance from the whole system around you would relentlessly pressurise you to conform. Your own organisation and its management (perhaps in some cases its owners or shareholders), the commissioners and regulators, the government and the whole social care establishment, with different motives that are often well-meant, would bear down on you to revert to your subservient and compliant former position. (And this is the case even when some of those who will put pressure on you to conform are at the same time supporting a development programme for managers.) There are and have been many examples of exceptionally good care services but by their nature they are isolated cases...yes, exceptional. On their own, individual efforts to lead change will not bring about the whole-system development that is needed. Only when managers join together as a professional body will the whole system of social care improve.

THE CARESHIRE SOCIAL CARE MANAGERS' NETWORK (CONTINUED FROM CHAPTER 6)

Gloria's proposal for a managers' network was accepted by The National Skills Academy for Social Care, and the funding was assured for the first ten meetings. Gloria made a modest bid for funding, which included room hire (at The Hub), refreshments and speakers' expenses. Gloria had already got the commitment of Gita, Gill and Geoff, and they had in turn contacted most of the social care managers in Careshire. They were particularly interested in welcoming managers of the smaller care homes for older people who are often not included in the meetings that already take place.

The exercise of gathering the network together was in itself very revealing. There was already a variety of meetings taking place. There were meetings of the local care association, attended principally by care home proprietors. Careshire social services held regular meetings for managers and proprietors at which the regulator, local authority commissioners, safeguarding specialists, and dementia and continence advisors addressed the attendees to tell them of any new developments in their specialisms. Managers from home care, learning and physical disabilities, mental health and substance misuse and care homes for older people rarely went to meetings with each other because they were seen to be different areas of work requiring very different skills and knowledge. There were also several training companies and colleges putting on courses – all geared to some sort of 'compliance' – for managers and other staff. And the larger care providers had meetings of their own managers, so Gita, for example, would go to a monthly meeting at her regional office where she met the managers from the other homes in her company. At none of these meetings did managers feel that they were in charge; they went because someone had something to tell them and, usually, this entailed something extra or different that they now had to do.

Gloria saw the network as an opportunity for managers to take the lead – to authorise themselves to lead. She, Gita, Gill and Geoff had already started working together. They shared with each other a very different attitude and approach. They were all prepared to challenge how things were now and they were committed to the clients of their services, and making their services work together to meet clients' needs. They found that they were connected through their clients and they quickly saw the services they managed as the local social service. So Mrs Smith, for instance, was a client who used three services at different times (4Cs, The Hub Club and The Limes); Edwin was a resident and community member at The Willows and worked at The Hub; Jean attended a Hub club, was supported by 4Cs and was a volunteer at The Limes; and, after she left The Willows, Martha was supported by 4Cs and was a volunteer at the Hub luncheon club. Gloria, Gita, Gill and Geoff, managing services that all had different external management structures, focused on the needs of their clients and created care to meet their needs. Careshire social services were very happy with this approach, although they had to fit the care that was arranged into a 'package' that could then be funded.

Gloria, Gita, Gill and Geoff reckoned that if they could operate like this, so could most of the other managers. At the first network meeting, attended by about 20 local managers, the four of them talked about their coordinated and collaborative way of working. They also described the support that they got from each other and how they were able to discuss some of the difficult issues that came up.

Initially, some of the network members wanted to invite the regulator and commissioners to address the meetings, but Gloria resisted the suggestion and was strongly supported. After the first getting to know each other and planning session, Gloria structured the meetings into two parts. During the first half, each member reported briefly about their work, issues that had come up and how they were feeling. Then the group divided into twos and threes and discussed these issues in detail, and then came back all together for ten minutes. In the second half, the whole network had a discussion, led by one or two members who introduced the subject for discussion.

To begin with, Gloria encouraged the self-selected twos and threes in the first session to be from different areas of the work. So, for example, someone wanting to discuss a staffing issue in a care home for people with physical disabilities would work with a home care manager and the manager of a small care home for older people. This mixing up of the client groups helped the managers to broaden their knowledge and outlook, recognise the commonalities, be open to different approaches and possibilities, and to develop consultancy and supervisory skills. As they gained confidence, members became more at ease with speaking of their work with colleagues from the same services (with the same client group) as them.

It didn't take long for close working relationships to be formed, and for members to be consulting with and supporting each other outside the network meetings.

In the second session, members began to develop their shared professional identity, their values, knowledge and skills. They also started to see the service they managed as part of a network of social care services to the wider community, and to be optimistic and ambitious about social care. They became more assertive and, in later meetings, they called in representatives from the regulator and from the commissioners to explore some of the issues that were coming up. This engagement was very different from the former subservient relationship.

Gloria organised a subgroup to discuss training issues including apprenticeships and student placements, both of which most managers wished to support and encourage, but which were proving problematic because colleges, universities and other training organisations were not playing their part. Before setting up any placement, college staff were expected to spend a whole day with the care organisation, familiarising themselves with the way the place worked and with its core task. The group met with the training providers to design training that was better suited to the core task.

Towards the end of the first set of network meetings, Careshire Health and Social Care Commissioning Support (a joint initiative from health and social care) invented a new auditing tool, which they called a 'care quality dashboard'. They proposed to make the satisfactory completion of the dashboard – asking all the questions the regulator also asked – a contractual obligation. In other words, providers would be forced to use it or their services would not be commissioned. The network called in the commissioners and the regulators and told them to sort it out because they were not going to duplicate 'quality monitoring' returns for two organisations that should be working together. The dashboard was withdrawn.

After three meetings, Gloria proposed that they should ask a group consultant to attend the remainder of this first series of network meetings to give some independent, external feedback to the group. Members learned about their own group process, their roles and the nature of leadership. This not only helped the network to stay on task but, as with the whole experience of the network development, members were able to take very practical ideas and leadership skills back to their own services.

The experience of the network meetings was transformational. Even before the end of the first series, the network was spawning new connections, collaborations and partnerships. With the experience of the network, several members were joining up for external supervision and people were visiting each other's services. Managers were using their own team meetings and staff supervision much more effectively. They now felt able to initiate developments in practice and had the confidence to propose changes to their own managers, proprietors and companies. They were no longer simply waiting to be told what to do.

Of course, they had four excellent examples of leadership in Gloria, Gita, Gill and Geoff on whom the launch and success of the network had initially depended. But their leadership drew out the latent leadership in members. After all, they had responded positively to the invitation to join, they had remained members and become active in the network, and their leadership spread to those managers who had declined the first invitation to join. Within a year over half the managers in the whole of Careshire had joined the network (two more networks were set up), and the network was developing into The Careshire Social Care Partnership, a network not just of individual managers, but of linked, collaborating services.

At the last meeting, the group reviewed their work and shared with each other the progress for themselves and for their services that had been made. Several people asked the rhetorical questions, 'Why did we just go along with things before? Why didn't we get together before?' They didn't expect to discuss these questions because the situation had now changed quite dramatically for them, but their consultant made one of her occasional interventions: 'So, why *did* you just go along with things, and why *didn't* you get together before?'

Time was running out; the group attempted to ignore these questions and hurried on to more (understandably) self-congratulatory appreciation of the network. Gita, with her background of organisation and system analysis and quick to pick up what was going on beneath the surface, brought the group back to the questions they had posed themselves, been reminded of and then tried to avoid considering.

The ensuing discussion included the following honest reflections:

- Life's easier if you've got someone telling you what to do and then you can blame them for whatever goes wrong.

- When you are on your own and the world seems to be against you, you just settle for survival.

- I didn't have to think before. I didn't have to argue with my proprietor. I just did my hours and got paid. No one complained.

- I was like an institutionalised resident. I had found a way to avoid facing up to myself. I didn't want anyone to disturb me and I certainly didn't want to look hard at what I was doing. This has been a liberating experience and I feel I've only just started.

- Oh well, I complained all the time to my family, to my team, to anybody except my manager, the regulator, the commissioners, or anyone else that I really needed to complain about and do something about. I just lived with it, but it was very unsatisfying and frustrating. I didn't feel I was really achieving anything…until I joined the network and you lot forced me to think what I could actually do to change things – but that was only with the support I got here.

- When I started out as a manager, I thought I would change everything, but then I just got weary of all the obstacles in my way, and I gave up.

- I was actually frightened when I came to the first network meeting. I didn't tell my regional manager. Then I was even more frightened when I realised what a responsibility it was starting to do my job the way it ought to be done, but now I'm really pleased I stuck with it. I'm not frightened any more; I'm excited and feel twice the person I was before. The feeling of the network around you, and the things we've already changed…and the effect it's already had on my team… I don't think anything will stop us now.

- If we don't remind ourselves of what it was like before, we could easily sink back into it. This leadership lark is hard work! We have to stick together but also stay self-critical. I think a little bit of complacency was creeping in!

- I didn't realise we had so much power. We don't have to do as we're told when we know it's not the right thing to do. We can really change social care. It's our job and at last we can start getting on with it.

There's really only one question left from this chapter: are you going to step up to leadership? Are you going to join up with other managers and lead good care?

AFTERWORD

As I finish writing this book, two new reports have just been published. Viewing the health service and local public services from different angles, coming to similar conclusions and making parallel recommendations, I'm pleased to see that they support much of what I have written here.

In *Reforming the NHS from within: Beyond Hierarchy, Inspection and Markets* (The King's Fund), Chris Ham argues that the best route to system-wide transformation is improvement from within, and that external reforms (targets, performance management, inspection and regulation, and competition and choice) have not worked. Change will come, not from politicians but locally from doctors, nurses and other NHS staff. Politicians should stop shifting direction and thereby creating barriers to change. Long-term improvement will come through commitment not compliance, and through investment in staff. Successful organisations depend on continuity of leadership, organisational stability, and clear vision and goals. Leadership needs to be 'collective and distributed'. Innovation will come from the integration of providers and systems.

And John Seddon, in partnership with Locality, has recently produced a report called *Saving Money by Doing the Right Thing: Why 'local by default' Must Replace 'diseconomies of scale'* in which he argues the case for local services that respond directly to people who need help. Services that 'assess rather than understand; transact rather than build relationships; refer on rather than take responsibility; prescribe packages of activity rather than take the time to understand what improves a life' are wasteful, ineffective and create 'failure demand'. The report proposes an alternative: 'public services should be "local by default"; they should help people to help themselves; they should focus on underlying purpose rather than outcomes, and they should manage value not cost'.

I have used John Seddon's systems analysis, and in particular his powerful concept of 'failure demand', throughout this book. Where organisations have engaged his consultancy (Vanguard) they have achieved remarkable changes.

After the writing was finished, but before this book went to print, John Kennedy of the Joseph Rowntree Foundation published his radical inquiry into care homes (www.jrf.org.uk/publications/john-kennedys-care-home-inquiry). His conclusions are plain and clear:

The underlying problems are ignored, unrecognised.

You can't tell people to be kind – you have to make the whole system kind.

…the people who give us our care need to be cared for and supported themselves.

Without the best managers, care homes can't succeed.

Care homes must be part of our communities and be able to contribute to our communities.

We must be able to understand better the difference between evil and a mistake. Our lives are risky, things go wrong.

Top-down, outside-in regulation is not working.

Far too little is done to ensure the fundamental conditions required to promote good care.

Where care homes are, what they do and how they fit into the wider economy is vital.

The messages from Kennedy at Joseph Rowntree, John Seddon at Vanguard, Chris Ham at The King's Fund and from many others including me, thinking about systems as I board the 109 bus to Brixton, take a while to be heard by government and the health and social care establishment. So improving social care, the task, heart and art of it, is down to you, the managers of care. You lead; the others will follow.

Appendix 1

ACTION LEARNING

Leading good care involves action learning. Good care grows out of action learning. A well-functioning care team learn together from action. In care work there is no true learning without action, and there can be no development in care without learning.

In handover meetings, the team report on their work; problems, issues and events are discussed; the team apply their collective thinking and they go back to work having learned from the discussion. In supervision, work is thought about, discussed and learned from, and the learning is taken forward in action. In team meetings and community meetings the same process takes place.

As a manager and leader, you will of course learn from action and act with that learning, but much of the time you will be facilitating the learning of your team and organisation. You need more. Like your team, you need to learn from and with your peers. You need a network of colleagues with whom you can learn from your actions as a manager and leader.

SETTING UP A NETWORK AND ACTION LEARNING SETS

Central to the National Skills Academy for Social Care Registered Managers' Programme is the principle of managers 'self-authorising' or moving from merely doing as they are told to taking authority and leading from the front, on task and on the ground. Effective care is *responsive*; in other words, care is given in response to people's needs (the core task). Leading a responsive service means giving care workers the *responsibility* and *authority* (and support) to engage directly with their clients and *respond* to need. This requires a systemic change in the structure, organisation and management of social care – from the ground up, not from the top down.

While such change can happen only if the top stops issuing insistent but inevitably ineffectual demands, it will be initiated, led and enacted by 20,000 or more managers. Without a good number of these managers taking the initiative (and being supported in taking it) the change we are seeking will not happen. So the top must allow and enable it to happen, but it can only be initiated and led by the managers on the ground.

The managers in the stories in this book (Gita, Gloria, Gill and Geoff) take the initiative to set up their own network to support and learn from each other, and to develop a comprehensive social care service in their locality.

What is an action learning set?

It is a group of people meeting regularly, bringing and sharing their work (events, experience, feelings, ideas) to be worked on with the rest of the group. Thereby, they are able to learn, reflect, review, plan and do. Action learning is a way of working that can be transferred to the organisations from which members come.

Principles and commitments of action learning sets (groups)

- Attendance is voluntary. Members are not directed to attend by their organisation; they decide to come for themselves.

- Each member is equal – there is no expert, no teacher, and everyone is entitled to equal time and attention.

- The group is work focused.

- Each member makes a commitment to learn and to make progress with their own *and* other members' work problems, issues and plans.

- Each member makes a commitment to the group to attend regularly, to share their knowledge, experience, ideas and skills, and to use their ignorance positively to listen and learn from the knowledge, experience, ideas and skills of others.

- All members of the set are responsible for the work they do together.

- What is brought to the group is confidential to the group.

What happens in an action learning set?

Action learning sets can take different forms; the members decide what form and can adjust and alter the process by agreement. The following is only one way of conducting an action learning set.

- A typical set would meet for half a day or an evening once a month with up to ten members.

- The set may start with a round robin of everyone checking in with how their work is going and how they are feeling.

- This could be followed by just one member telling the group in some depth about a particular aspect of work that they want the group to work on with them. The rest of the group ask questions that help the presenter to clarify and explore, and to open up thought and understanding. Some questions can be answered and some just thought about.

- That is followed by a discussion amongst everyone except the member who presented the issue. So the member listens and learns from the ideas, analysis and perception of the others.

- Then the member who presented has a short time to tell the group what they've learned, understood and gained from the discussion and the plans that they've been formulating while they've been listening.

- And the set is closed by every member briefly checking out with what they've learned from the session and what they are going do with it at work.

Sets can be themed. So, for example, systemic leadership could form an additional part of the set meeting. The chapters and stories in this book could be used by a set as the basis for one half of a meeting, while the other half concentrates on the issues that the members bring.

Facilitation

People who already have some experience of this type of learning may be able to run their own action learning sets without a facilitator by taking turns or by sharing the facilitation throughout. Alternatively – and more usually – the set will have a facilitator to take care of the process for them, and to offer feedback about the process. (For example, the group and its process/relationships are likely to reflect some of the material that is brought by the members.)

Action learning is a powerful process and it is transferrable. Managers who set up networks and action learning sets will take the model back to the service they lead, and together they will form a formidable force for change and development in social care.

Appendix 2

HUMPTY DUMPTY'S SOCIAL CARE WORDS AND PHRASES

'When I use a word,' Humpty Dumpty said, in rather a scornful tone,
'it means just what I choose it to mean—neither more nor less.'

(Lewis Carroll, *Through the Looking Glass*)

Taking their cue from Humpty Dumpty, the Commission for Social Care Inspection (CSCI), the former regulator of social care in England, called their planned inspections 'random inspections'. Random means lacking any prearranged plan. Of course, the meanings of words evolve through usage, and some do come to mean the exact opposite of their original meaning, but neither Humpty Dumpty nor CSCI, in their infantile delusions of omnipotence, could successfully bring about such a change by decree. And even if few people are willing to say so at the time for fear of retaliation, such a mixture of wilfulness, ignorance and arrogance leaves the perpetrator open to ridicule.

The words we use do matter. Words are metaphors or, as Keats described them: 'images of thoughts refined'. We use them to think and communicate: about people, things, actions, ideas, events. They carry with them history, feelings and attitudes; cultures and beliefs. A useful or striking phrase used repeatedly or indiscriminately soon becomes a cliché, yet there is always meaning lurking beneath the most banal statements.

Even the most impersonal writing matters to the person who wrote it. Any criticism of one's writing can therefore feel like a personal attack. Some of the words and phrases and their usage that I am drawing attention to, questioning and sometimes making fun of are used by friends and colleagues whom I like and respect for their contribution to social care, and I am not trying to alienate or offend them.

When we hear or read phrases such as 'world class commissioning', 'delivering better outcomes', or 'driving up quality', we should think about and question the history and the overt and covert meanings of the words. What are they trying to convey? In whose interests is it to express this idea in this way? And what hidden anxieties are being suppressed?

In writing this book, I have chosen every word and combination of words. I have read and reread, and changed thousands of the words and sentences I first wrote. And I know that I still will not always have expressed what I intended to express. Yet what I did not intend to express and what I did intend to imply, but by slyly written hints and winks, may reveal themselves to readers. When we read, we read between the lines and we look for the subtext. As with the spoken word, the writer implies and the reader infers. We pick up the tone. An underlying meaning is sometimes very subtle and may be more in the mind of the reader than of the writer, and sometimes it's very obvious. So in rereading my paragraph above, in which I liken The Commission for Social Care Inspection to Humpty Dumpty, my feelings and attitudes towards the widely esteemed (there I go again) former regulator for England are plain to see.

'Service users', 'people who use services', 'clients', 'residents', 'customers', 'citizens': each of these words and phrases carries with it a history and meaning. Some – such as 'service users' – are used to avoid others that carry with them negative connotations. So 'client' originated in social work as a way of according respect to the person and professionalism to the social worker, but then fell out of favour because in use it was seen as describing a person without power in relation to the powerful professional. In addition, social workers (especially with adults) were no longer 'case workers' but more 'care managers' or 'brokers' finding practical 'packages' of support rather than practising psychosocial case work. 'User' came into favour (in spite of the parallel with drug user) because it was seen to be more neutral, but gives the 'service user' an active role with more power and choice. Service user quickly became 'SU' in some social care organisations. So the regulator led the way with 'people who use services', which in turn has begun to wane in popularity, partly because it's such a mouthful and doesn't bear too much repetition. So here I am using the word 'client' in the interests of brevity and, I have to admit, as a slightly mischievous challenge. It is the role of a writer to stimulate discussion.

With many words – as with acronyms – we are discouraged from stopping and thinking by a familiarity that skates over meaning and content. Big – but not necessarily long – words, such as 'risk', 're-ablement' and 'co-production' are bandied around at a meeting as if everyone using them knew and agreed on the meaning.

We should think about all the following words and phrases. We should question their use and meaning and, even if we continue to use them, we should try not to fall into the lazy habit of simply following fashion or the timid habit of not asking what is meant.

'**Ensure**' – one of the most overused and often redundant words. It means to make certain or to guarantee. A notice on a double-decker coach warns passengers not to fall down the stairs: 'For your own safety please ensure you use the handrails at all times.' The notice conjures up an image of an ageing group of passengers, faces drawn and anxious, their clothes turning to rags with the passage of time, still gripping the handrail for their own safety years after they first complied with the written instructions. 'Ensure' is such a popular word now that it creeps in everywhere. On the same coach, the courier asks passengers at the end of their journey to 'ensure' that they take all their 'personal' possessions with them. With uncharacteristic concision, she fails to add that you may leave behind your impersonal possessions. But, in social care, 'ensure' is not only unnecessary, it is used to promise what can't be delivered. No one can 'ensure the delivery of quality care', or 'safety', or everlasting happiness! So we shouldn't claim we can.

'**Around**' is a favourite fudge word. Someone may describe their job as working around adult abuse, alcohol, mental health, etc. It always seems to me that, if they are working around an issue, they may be either avoiding or missing the target.

'**Complaint**' – oh yes, we take all complaints very seriously…in fact, we've set up procedures and a whole new department that deals with complaints, so you don't have to. (Failure demand.)

'**Putting procedures in place**' – perhaps in a special file for the inspector to read? We keep it on the top shelf in the office where no one can reach it. And then we have another file to '**evidence**' that we have '**followed procedures**' (whether we really have or not) and that is for the inspector to examine as well. In this case the 'evidence' is the record we keep to ensure that something has been done, or at least has been recorded as done.

'**Open door policy**' is a rather grand way of saying you can come in and talk to me whenever you like, but it may mean I quite like being distracted from what I'm meant to be doing, and I don't like to commit myself to a proper supervision session.

'**Co-production**' is a good idea (sharing the creation of support between those who provide it and those who need it) but it is social care jargon and therefore counterproductive.

'WHITE VAN CARE': 'DRIVING' AND 'DELIVERING PACKAGES' OF 'QUALITY CARE'

The implication of many social care words and phrases is that care can be ordered, packaged, driven and delivered and paid for as if it were a thing, a commodity and not a human relationship. Thinking about care as merchandise, untouched by human heart, protects those who manage and administer care from the feelings that are associated with caring. And the whole notion of **'quality'** and **'quality ratings'** arises from the same thinking – the world of manufacturing, packaging, driving and delivering. When an organisation wants to sound **'robust'** and determined, it uses words such as **'driving (up)'** and **'delivery'**…all **'going forward'** of course. Even **'agendas'** are **'driven'**: the **'dignity agenda'**, the **'personalisation agenda'**, the **'quality agenda'**; they are all being driven hither and thither, but I've not seen one of them **'delivered'** yet. **'Action plans'** are delivered, and you might expect that to mean that the plan was carried out, but it more often means that the written action plan was delivered to the person who asked for it. Notice how new technocratic and macho words and phrases – such as **'dashboard'**, **'drilling down'**, **'deep diving'**, **'mainstreaming'**, **'close of play'** – keep being introduced, all to separate us from the difficult, messy, uncertain, emotional business of person-to-person care.

TOY TRAIN SET MANAGEMENT

I first thought of this phrase when I was consulting to a care home where the very inexperienced chief executive of the voluntary organisation that ran the home 'played' at his job as if the home was his toy train set. He had no understanding of care but liked to **'performance manage'** the manager, buy any new technology that appealed to him and sit at his computer having his lunch brought to him by the chef. He was immature, ignorant and completely unnecessary. The home's manager was very capable but he spoiled everything she tried to do. I still have a mental image – a fantasy – of him grabbing his toy engine from the manager and stamping his foot, yelling, 'It's mine. You're not allowed to play with it,' and throwing it on the floor.

There follow two examples of health and social care gobbledegook. The first (with my emphasis) is taken directly from the Department of Health (England) writing about 'world class commissioning'. The second takes us back to Careshire, the fictional setting of the stories in this book. However, as with Careshire, it is based on a real report from a local authority and uses many of the same 'Humpty Dumpty' words and phrases that were used in the original.

> The **world class commissioning** programme is **transforming** the way health and care services are commissioned. World class commissioning will **deliver** a more **strategic** and long-term approach to commissioning services, with a clear focus on delivering **improved health outcomes**. There are four **key elements** to the programme; a **vision** for world class commissioning, a set of world class commissioning **competencies**, an **assurance system** and a **support and development framework**.
>
> (From the Department of Health website, 7 April 2010)

While the Careshire Social Care Partnership was organising very personal, integrated care by focusing on the core task and pooling their resources to collaborate, central government were attempting to achieve similar results by funding a national agency to promote their 'personalisation agenda'. Local authorities were obliged to follow this central guidance, setting up their own personalisation units to meet the objectives of the national 'agenda'. Meanwhile government money for health and social care was being reduced. Finding themselves yet again squeezed between highfaluting proclamations of the government and being starved of funds by the same government, Careshire County Council issued empty statements about their personalisation programme dressed up to sound as if they were doing something. They were so preoccupied with meeting the central government requirements (linked to funding) that they were unaware that the Careshire Social Care Partnership, led by the network of local social care managers, was already achieving the objectives that the county council was obliged – but failing – to meet.

In a public response to questions from the central personalisation agency (**'Think neighbourhood and personalise'**), Careshire issued the following statement to account for the shortcomings in their **'TrueCare'** programme, using the phraseology of the national 'agenda':

> It was quite straightforward to select our **key priorities**, closely aligned with our **vision** of a **connected population**, where everyone in Careshire has the opportunity to be healthy and happy, and to prosper.
>
> We implemented our **action plan** and then waited three months so that we could reflect on progress against the eighteen actions which had been set against the three most **'under performing'** strands taken from the original **TrueCare** consultation.

We proceeded by selecting a **key action** from each of the original strands, and made these our **TrueCare** priorities.

Staying faithful to the county council's vision to increase the independence, health, happiness and prosperity of all Careshire citizens, we identified a need to **enhance practice quality** and to further **embed** the principles of **personalised support planning** around the adult social care workforce. By conducting a **case file audit and consultation**, we have ascertained that, although **people who use services** and carers are increasingly using direct payments to **purchase** their care and support, the evidence suggests that people need to be **further enabled** to have more choice and control through use of **person-centred approaches** to achieve independence and to **meet their goals**.

The increased use of direct payments points to a growing need to raise awareness with the public about the process of employing a personal assistant **(PA)**. Currently, our **CareFinder PA Register is under-utilised** – just 10 per cent of PAs employed are registered. We are therefore putting various **support mechanisms** in place in order to optimise the match between people with a direct payment and the registered PAs.

In accordance with our **vision to ensure** that the people of Careshire feel safer, happier and more supported in and by their neighbourhoods and communities, we have initiated a neighbourhood scheme, building relational capacity between individuals, local organisations and the public sector to **progress collective activity** through use of existing assets. Our approach is an **Asset-Based Community Development (ABCD)** approach which will enable participants to **access the information** they need from their own neighbourhoods and communities, thereby reducing dependence on public health and care services.

We expect **'mainstreaming'** will be the major potential issue in the ongoing **implementation** of the **TrueCare** programme. Mainstreaming in a large local authority such as Careshire is difficult enough, however we anticipate further difficulties in convincing both the public and **co-production** organisations that our **action plan** commitments are authentic. During phase one of the consultation, we were concerned to receive a number of comments from residents about the depth of our commitment to the project, and other professionals raised concerns about there being simply too many initiatives across the various organisations.

Going forward, we would welcome fresh input from **Think Neighbourhood and Personalise around** offering ways in which to provide further support to organisations which are committed to **delivering on** these action plans.

Did anything happen? If so, what? I think we've gone round in a big, wordy circle and ended up where we began. I wonder what the people who live in this local authority and pay for this to be written make of it.

BOOKS AND OTHER RESOURCES

I have listed below a small selection of books and resources, all of which I have read or used and can recommend. There are many others waiting for you to find your own way to.

BOOKS

First are some of the books that have influenced me in my work in social care and underpin much of the theory and ideas in this book. I include my own books. Reading or dipping into any of these books will help you to understand social care at a deeper level.

Robert de Board, *The Psychoanalysis of Organizations*, Routledge, 1978.

John Burton, *The Handbook of Residential Care*, Routledge, 1993.

John Burton, *Managing Residential Care*, Routledge, 1998.

Centre for Policy on Ageing, *Home* Life, CPA, 1984.

Roger Clough, *The Practice of Residential Work*, Macmillan, 2000.

Stanley Cohen, *Visions of Social Control*, Polity Press, 1985.

Tim Dartington, *Managing Vulnerability*, Karnac, 2010.

Department of Health, *Homes Are For Living In*, HMSO, 1989.

John Harris and Des Kelly, *Management Skills in Social Care*, Gower, 1991

Clare Huffington, David Armstrong, William Halton, Linda Hoyle and Jane Pooley (eds), *Working Below the Surface*, Karnac, 2004.

Howard Jones, *The Residential Community*, Routledge and Keegan Paul, 1979.

Tom Kitwood, *Dementia Reconsidered*, Open University Press, 1997.

Michael Mandelstam, *How We Treat the Sick*, Jessica Kingsley Publishers, 2011.

Peter Marris, *Loss and Change*, Routledge and Keegan Paul, 1986.

Isabel Menzies Lyth, *Containing Anxiety in Institutions*, Free Association Books, 1988.

Lyth's book contains the clearest and most important insight into how health and social care systems work: 'The functioning of social systems as a defence against anxiety' is the best primer for understanding what is 'beneath the surface'.

Gareth Morgan, *Images of Organization*, Sage, 1986.

National Institute for Social Work, *A Positive Choice*, HMSO, 1988.

Anton Obholzer and Vega Zagier Roberts (eds), *The Unconscious at Work*, Routledge, 1994.

Lionel F. Stapley, *Individuals, Groups, and Organizations Beneath the Surface*, Karnac, 2006.

Adrian Ward, *Working in Group Care*, BASW/Policy Press, 2007.

Donald W. Winnicott, *Playing and Reality*, Penguin, 1971.

Second are some practical books.

The Social Care Manager's Handbook: A Practical Guide for Registered Managers and All Leaders in Social Care Services.

Published and updated annually by The National Skills Academy for Social Care, this is an indispensable guide to everyday management of social care. If you join the National Skills Academy for Social Care Registered Managers' Programme (see below) you will get a free copy with your membership.

Penny Henderson, Jim Holloway and Anthea Millar, *Practical Supervision*, Jessica Kingsley Publishers, 2014.

Graham Hopkins, *Plain English for Social Services*, Russel House Publishing, 1998.

Buz Loveday, *Leadership for Person-Centred Dementia Care*, Jessica Kingsley Publishers, 2012.

Mike Pedler, *Action Learning for Managers*, Lemos and Crane, 1996.

Stephen Stirk and Helen Sanderson, *Creating Person-Centred Organisations*, Jessica Kingsley Publishers, 2012.

Jessica Kingsley publish a wide selection of books on all aspects of social care.

JOURNALS AND MAGAZINES

I have been writing for *Caring Times*, which is published monthly, for many years. Most recently, I have written two series of articles: 'Care Workers' Dilemmas' and 'It Ain't Necessarily So'. These articles (40) set out everyday issues that confront care workers and managers and can be used in team discussions and training. They are available at: www.careinfo.org

Care Management Matters.

Journal of Care Services Management.

Journal of Social Work Practice (Journal of GAPS – the Group for the Advancement of Psychodynamics and Psychotherapy in Social Work).

Organisational and Social Dynamics (OPUS – see below).

WEBSITES AND NEWSLETTERS

Community Care e-newsletters – a good way of keeping in touch with all developments and news in social care. www.communitycare.co.uk

Healthcare Review is an excellent weekly digest of all social care news edited by Keith Lewin, a partner in Brunswicks Law Firm. www.brunswicks.eu

Joseph Rowntree Foundation has a library of interesting and influential reports. Here you will find John Kennedy's Care Home Inquiry. www.jrf.org.uk

My Home Life is a movement that promotes quality of life for those living, dying, visiting and working in care homes, and the website provides a wide variety of positive and practical ideas. www.myhomelife.org.uk

Vanguard Consulting (John Seddon) has a superb website for everyone interested in systems thinking and systemic change. www.systemsthinking.co.uk

MEMBERSHIP ORGANISATIONS

I strongly encourage you to join The National Skills Academy for Social Care Registered Managers' Programme. The more managers who join, the more power we will create together – the more authority we will have – to lead change and improvement in social care. www.nsasocialcare.co.uk/registered-managers

OPUS is an organisation for promoting understanding of society. I have been an OPUS Associate for many years. OPUS encourages a reflective understanding of societies by an approach based on group relations, psychoanalysis, and systems theory and practice. Through a mainly experiential approach, OPUS provides conferences, scientific meetings, workshops and listening posts that encourage members to go beyond the obvious and to seek an understanding of the underlying dynamics affecting societies. OPUS also publishes an excellent journal *Organisational and Social Dynamics* (see above). www.opus.org.uk

INDEX

abuse
  and BBC *Panorama* (2014) 76
  and compliance 82
  and diversion from the core task 43
  potential for 77
  protection from 145–6
  scandals 18, 41
action learning sets 21, 26, 142, 190–3
anxiety 63
  and dependency 66–8
  defences against 75–6, 79, 86, 141
Association of Care Managers 17
avoidance 83, 133, 139

bad feelings 76–7, 145–6
branding 31, 41, 57
Bristol University 17
Brixton 13–15
bullying 82–3, 146

care home(s)
  admission to 121
  as 'container' 65
  community meetings 130–1
  core task 40
  daily life 91–2
  failing 138
  finances 136
  handovers 129
  notices 132
  office work 51
  room boundary 95
  specialist 59
care plan(s)
  and the core task 120
  and home care 146
  and personalisation 78
  and routines 69
Castlebeck 41, 75
class 34–5
collusion 67, 83, 166, 178

commissioning
  and home care 171
  and local authorities 42–3, 111
  and personalisation 122
  'world class commissioning' 194, 197–8
Community Service Volunteer 17
complaints 196
  and 'failure demand' 47–9, 157–9
  and the role of the regulator 147
compliance 82–3, 118
  the antithesis of leadership 178
  and the core task 43–5, 50
  hiding beneath 171
  and inspection 44
  and medication 143–4
  and organisational defences 70
  and quality assurance 125
  and risk aversion 79
consultancy 17, 20, 55, 180
Croydon 14
CSCI (Commission for Social Care
    Inspection) 194
culture 18, 34–5, 67, 124
  compliance culture 17
  glitzy culture 84
  healthy culture 143
  learning culture 90–1, 151–3
  participative culture 125–6
  shared culture 144
  staff room culture 70
  top-down culture 171
  work culture 90

death 83, 86, 92, 98
decisions 19, 75, 124, 127–8, 171
  and boundary 95–116
  and community meetings 130–1
  and money 131, 135–7
  and risk assessments 79
defence(s) 61–86, 141, 176

dependency 66–7
dignity 45, 119, 158–9
    'agenda' 197

Establishment, the 18
    social care establishment 77, 159, 189
    perpetuating a failing system 174
    pressure to conform 183

'failure demand' 43, 45, 102
    consuming resources 177, 188
    and complaints 196
    downward defensive spiral 47–50
    an endemic disease 157–60
finance and budgeting 135–7
    control of 32, 41, 51
    and the whole task 52–3
    individual 78
Frogmore 17

garden(s), gardening 31, 38, 39

handover(s) 87, 89, 129–30, 190
head office 31–2, 51, 81–2, 138
    and core task 176
    and recruitment 100
    relationship with 139, 141, 171
home care
    clients' feedback 125
    'containment' 65
    examples 25, 101–5, 109–10, 127–9,
        151–2, 160–2, 170–1
    expertise 58
    'in the community' 29
    meetings 89
    listening 92
    practical support 52
    underpaid, exploited staff 38, 146
housekeeping 32, 52, 140

improvement agencies 54–5, 85
incontinence 67, 74, 158
inspection see regulation and inspection

local authority
    contract monitoring 77
    core task 42–3
    cuts 32, 33, 123
    and failure demand 49–50
    fees and funding 110–11
    gobbledegook 198–9
    loss 63–4, 67, 83, 84, 86, 119, 176

medication 69, 143–4
    errors 47
    monitoring 50, 70, 159

National Skills Academy for Social Care
    23–4, 172, 174, 190

occupancy rates 32, 42
OPUS 22, 202, 203

Panorama 41, 46, 75, 76, 77
pay and wages 32, 35, 77
personalisation 78–9, 122–4, 197, 198
Platt, Denise 11
power 15, 98
    and authority 119, 179
    and office work 81–2
    and 'client' 195
    collective 202
    to dismiss 172
    to transform 112
procedure(s) 14, 43, 58, 61, 67–9, 78–80,
        85–6
    and abuse 145
    and medication 143–4
    'putting procedures in place' 16, 45,
        74–5, 196
    reactive 158

quality assurance 15, 125–6
    and the manager's boundaries 96
    and the core task 41
    procedures 75, 158

record keeping (example) 50–1, 158, 181
regulation and inspection 22, 43–6, 75, 85,
        144, 146–8, 175, 188, 194
reputation 42, 110–13, 133, 142
Richard Cusden Homes, The 17
risk assessment(s) 71, 79

safeguarding 45 (example), 47–9, 70, 106,
        145–6, 159
Savile, Sir James Wilson Vincent 18
School for Advanced Urban Studies 17
School for Social Entrepreneurs 17
Seddon, John (Vanguard Consulting) 23, 43,
        157, 188, 189, 202
self-authorising 19, 23–4, 190
'Social Care Compact' 85
social ecology 38
specialisation 30, 59, 80–1, 177
Stafford General Hospital 18

staff selection 96, 99–100
standards 43–5, 50, 85, 123, 147
supervision 54, 86, 88, 89–91, 145, 182
   organising 139
   recording 133

Tavistock (Institute and Clinic) 17, 22
The Big Red Book 14
theory 22–3, 61, 91, 136
therapeutic community 22, 25, 32, 36, 39,
     131, 165, 171
The Social Care Manager's Handbook 20, 22,
     24, 118, 146, 201
toy train set (management) 16, 17, 197
training 54–6, 90–1, 174–5
Transport for London 14

vulnerability 36, 63–7, 84, 86, 180

Winterbourne View 18, 41, 46, 47, 75

Young, Michael 17